Photo courtesy of the Missouri History
Museum/Library and Research Center

# Saint Louis Italians
## The Hill and Beyond

By Eleanore Berra Marfisi

G. Bradley Publishing,Inc. • St. Louis, Missouri, 63122

## PUBLICATION STAFF

Author . . . . . . . Eleanore Berra Marfisi
Production Coordinator . . .Blake Baraks
Restaurant Profiles . . . . . .Gloria Baraks
Editors . . . . . . . . . . . . . Gloria Baraks
                                 Liz Roy
                                 Diane Gannon
Food Photography . . . . . Voyles Studio:
                                 Jim Kersting
                                 Darlene Weber
                                 Kyle Weber
Additional Photography . . Josh Monken
Recipe Editor . . . . . . . . Janice Denham
Photo Editor. . . . . . . . Michael Bruner
Book Design. . . . . . . . . Diane Kramer
Dust Jacket Design . . . . Michael Bruner
Editors' Assistants. . . . . . . . Tori Urban
                                 Sonya Spence
Publisher. . . G. Bradley Publishing, Inc.

**End Sheets:**
Front: (Left) A living Christmas Crèche at Our Lady Help
of Christians Church. (Right) Biddle at 13th Street, looking
north in St. Louis' Little Italy neighborhood.
Back: Food shots courtesy of LoRusso's Cucina,
Lombardo's Restaurant, and Marconi Bakery.

## DEDICATION

*It is with overwhelming pride that
I dedicate this book to my mother,
Maria Anna Alberti (see story, page
64). She came as a young girl to a
land of which she knew very little,
and persevered, raising a family of
ten children. With moral resolve
and a loving, yet determined,
spirit, she set a course for future
generations to emulate. Her example
is representative of the many early
Italian immigrants who have made
indispensable contributions to the
City of St. Louis.*

*– Eleanore Berra Marfisi*

*Maria Anna Alberti*

*Go to www.gbradleypublishing.com
for other ethnic cookbooks of interest.*

*Italian St. Louis*
by Eleanore Berra Marfisi

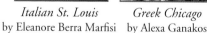
*Greek Chicago*
by Alexa Ganakos

*German Milwaukee*
by Trudy Paradis

*Polish Chicago*
by Joseph Zurawski

*The Foods of
Chicago*

*I Remember Nonna*
by Eleanore Berra Marfisi

ISBN 978-0-9774512-6-5
Printed in the U.S.A.

# TABLE OF CONTENTS

Foreword by Monsignor Polizzi .........................5

HISTORY:

Notable Italians ............................................6

Notable Italian Americans ...............................8

Notable St. Louis Italians ..............................14

The Story of Little Italy.................................22

Fratellanza...............................................32

Produce Row..............................................34

Italians at 1904 World's Fair............................37

The Clay Mines...........................................38

The Hill.................................................40

**Familiar Places:**

    Joe Fassi's ......................................44

    Rosciglione Bakery ...............................45

    Vitale's Bakery ..................................46

    Viviano's Festa Italiano .........................47

    Milo's Bocce Garden..............................48

    Marconi Bakery...................................49

    Hill Top Inn .....................................50

Old Memories & Old Friends ..............................51

History of Italian Restaurants...........................65

Ruggeri's................................................74

St. Louis Pizza .........................................77

**ITALIAN RESTAURANTS OF ST. LOUIS:**

**Bartolino's** ..........................................82

    • Australian Barramundi in Crazy Water

    • Chicken Franciacorta

**Café Napoli** ..........................................88

    • Rigatoni Sorrentina

    • Veal Chop Vino Rosso

**Charlie Gitto's Downtown** .............................94

    • Pasta Messina

    • Steak Francesca

**Del Pietro's** ........................................100

    • Parmesan-Encrusted Pork Chop

    • Sfinci

**Gian-Tony's** .........................................106

    • Chicken Cannelloni

    • Scallops Capriccio

**John Mineo's** ........................................112

    • Sicilian Stuffed Artichoke Appetizer

    • Mare E Monte

**Kemoll's** ............................................118

    • Filet Douglas

    • Shrimp Artichoke Moutarde

**Lombardo's** ..........................................124

    • Italian Sausage a la Lombardo

    • Veal Saltimbocca

**Lorenzo's** ...........................................130

    • Ricotta Cheesecake

    • Gnocchi

**LoRusso's Cucina** ....................................136

    • Cioppino

    • Crawfish and Andouille Fettucine

**The Pasta House Co.** .................................142

    • Chicken Spiedini

    • Mediterranean Seafood Pasta

**Paul Manno's** ........................................148

    • Rigatoni Arrabiata

    • Veal Panna

**Pietro's** ............................................154

    • Breast of Chicken Maria

    • Sole Sebastian

**Portabella** ..........................................160

    • Crispy Scallops

    • Eggplant Tower

**Rich & Charlie's** ....................................166

    • Rich & Charlie's Salad

    • Pasta con Broccoli

**Rigazzi's** ...........................................172

    • Chicken Giambetti

    • Pasta Sienna

**Tony's** .............................................178

    • Honey-Glazed Figs with Gorgonzola

    • Seared Scallops with Black Truffles

**Trattoria Marcella** ..................................184

    • Polenta Fries

    • Lobster Risotto

**Yacovelli's** .........................................190

    • Brasciole

    • Parmesan-Encrusted Tilapia

**Zia's** ..............................................196

    • Linguine Carbonara

    • Pasta Tuttomare

**Dominic Galati**

The Perfect Italian Dinner/

Fall & Winter...........................................202

    • Appetizer of Shrimp

    • Spinach Soup with Chicken

    • Fettucine

    • Lemon Ice with Campari

    • Grilled Beef with Wild Mushroom Sauce

    • Insalata Mista con Formaggi

    • Crème Brulé

**Charlie Gitto, Jr.**

The Perfect Italian Dinner/

Summer & Spring ........................................208

    • Prosciutto with Melon

    • Sicilian Stuffed Artichoke

    • Grilled Summer Vegetables

    • Tomato Eggplant Stack

    • Veal Milanese

    • Zabaglione with Summer Berries

**Acknowledgements** ....................................214

**Contributors**........................................215

**Resources** ..........................................215

**Epilogue** ...........................................216

*Pictured is the wait staff, many of them future restaurateurs, at Tony's in the mid-1960s.*

# FOREWORD BY MONSIGNOR POLIZZI

I am the product of three worlds…my heritage…my community…and my faith; they are the bridges that span my life.

My Italian immigrant parents taught me the value of education and endowed me with a very strong work ethic. They had no formal education, but they possessed great wisdom. My brothers and sisters and I were taught to always do our best. My mother served as the best example; although she did not speak English and had limited education, she successfully managed a large restaurant. After tirelessly working for hours, she would come home and cook for our family. And I must say, she made us gourmet meals out of nothing! But most of all she taught us great lessons simply by her example…to work hard…to help one another, and to love God and family.

My faith is a great source of strength. Early education at Our Lady Help of Christians Church in Little Italy downtown encouraged me to enter the priesthood. The people in my parish were my extended family, not simply a community in which I lived.

Every neighbor, every store owner (and there were many) looked out for us kids in the neighborhood. They protected all of us as if we were their own.

We dared not get into trouble because out parents would find out even before we got home. The neighborhood looked upon that as their moral duty! I suppose it was what kept us in line.

Our parish community was like a small town nestled in the heart of a big city. Our church was the epicenter of our lives, activities, and entertainment. Procession, church, bazaars, and fireworks were regular summer Sunday afternoon enjoyment. Our Lady Help of Christians Church was the glue that held our community together. We were all family!

As a priest my mission took me to the Hill and St. Ambrose Church became my other extended family. I was determined to become a priest for the people, not simply a pulpit or desk minister. Spending time walking the streets and visiting homes on the Hill put me in touch with the community I have grown to know and to love.

Since I witnessed the demise of my wonderful downtown "Little Italy" neighborhood, I was determined not to let this happen to the Hill. They must be able to protect their community; they needed motivation and leadership to keep the neighborhood viable.

In 1964, we formed Hill 2000 because we planned on the Hill being there in the year 2000. It is now 2008, and we continue to thrive.

I suppose it is the pride and passion of the people that encourages me in all I do. Fierce pride in my Italian heritage, faith and family nourished the passion that supports my endeavors. These bridges continue to span my life.

One need only to look around St. Louis, visit the Italian restaurants and delis, walk through the streets of the Hill, stop and talk to Hill people, laugh with them, and you will understand what I feel.

*At left, Monsignor Polizzi's family. Above is Monsignor Polizzi outside St. Ambrose Church.*

# NOTABLE ITALIANS

The inhabitants of Italy, this wonderfully narrow peninsula, are as diverse as its geological composition. Although relatively diminuitive in size, the influence Italy has had on world culture is incalculable. The natural formations of the country vary from the magnificent Piedmont Mountains in the north to the rolling hills of Tuscany, then down through the verdant shores of Sicily. These distinct regions, and their various natural resources, have helped to mold the artistic and cultural uniqueness of her inhabitants.

**Cicero** [106 BC-43 BC] was a Roman statesman and philosopher, widely considered one of Rome's greatest orators and prose stylists.

**Virgil** [70 BC-19 BC] was a classical Roman poet and author of a twelve-book poem, the *Aeneid*, which became the Roman Empire's national epic.

**Ovid** [43 BC-17 AD], who wrote on love, abandoned women, and mythological transformations, had a decisive influence on European art and literature for centuries.

**Titus** [59 BC-17 AD] was a Roman historian who wrote *Ab Urbe Condita*, of Rome's founding (753 BC) through the reign of Caesar Augustus, the first emperor of the Roman empire.

**Julius Caesar** [100 BC-44 BC], Roman military and political leader, played a key role in transforming the Roman Republic into an Empire, extending all the way to the Atlantic Ocean.

**Marcus Aurelius** [121 AD-180] was a Stoic philospher and Roman Emperor from 161 to 180. His work *Meditations* is still revered as a literary monument to a government of service and duty.

**Constantine the Great** [272-337], Roman Emperor, was best known as the first Christian Emperor, issuing the Edict of Milan in 313, proclaiming religious tolerance in the Empire.

**Saint Francis of Assisi** [1181-1226], Roman Catholic founder of the Franciscans, was known as the patron saint of animals, birds, and Italy.

**Saint Thomas Aquinas** [1225-1274] was a Catholic priest in the Dominican Order. He is considered by many Catholics to be the Church's greatest theologian and philosopher.

**Giotto** [1267-1337], painter and architect, is the first in a line of great artists who contributed to the Renaissance.

**Brunelleschi** [1377-1446] was one of the foremost architects of the Renaissance. His principal work was the design for the dome of the Cathedral of Florence, Italy.

**Donatello** [1386–1466] Renaissance artist and sculptor from Florence.

**Botticelli** [1445-1510] was a painter under the patronage of Lorenzo de Medici. *The Birth of Venus* and *Primavera* rank now among the most familiar masterpieces of Florentine art.

**Leonardo da Vinci** [1452-1519] Scientist, mathematician, engineer, inventor, anatomist, painter, sculptor, architect, botanist, musician, and writer. He is widely considered to be one of the greatest painters of all time, known primarily for the *Mona Lisa* and *The Last Supper*, and perhaps the most diversely talented person ever to have lived.

**Michelangelo** [1475-1564] - Renaissance painter, sculptor, architect, poet, and engineer. Best known for his work in the Vatican where he painted the ceiling of the Sistine Chapel and designed the massive dome covering St. Peter's Basilica. Two of his best-known sculptures, the *Pietà* and the *David*, were created before he turned 30.

**Vivaldi** [1678-1741] was a Venetian priest and Baroque music composer. *The Four Seasons*, a series of four violin concerti, is his best-known work.

**Paganini** [1782-1840], a composer, was one of the most celebrated violin virtuosi of his time, and one of the pillars of modern violin technique.

**Puccini** [1858-1924] was a composer whose operas, *La Bohème*, *Tosca*, and *Madama Butterfly*, are among the most frequently performed.

**Enrico Caruso** [1873-1921] One of the greatest tenors in history, Caruso was also the most popular singer, in any genre, in the first two decades of the 20th Century. With over 260 recordings, he was truly a pioneer of the record industry.

**Luciano Pavarotti** [1935-2007] was a tenor, who crossed over into popular music and became one of the world's most famous vocal performers.

NOVA ITALIÆ DELINEATIO

**Antonio Stradivari** [1644-1737] was a luthier (a crafter of stringed instruments such as violins, cellos, guitars, and harps). Stradivari is generally considered the most significant artisan in this field.

**Dante** [1265-1321] His work, the *Divine Comedy*, is regarded as the greatest literary work composed in the Italian language and a masterpiece of world literature. Dante is also referred to as the "Father of the Italian Language."

**Petrarch** [1304-1374], an Italian Renaissance scholar and poet, is often called the "Father of Humanism." Credited with developing the sonnet, Petrarch was also known for being one of the first people to call the Middle Ages the Dark Ages.

**Marco Polo** [1254–1324] Venetian trader and explorer, Marco Polo's description of the Far East and its riches inspired Christopher Columbus to try to reach Asia by sea, in a westward route.

**Christopher Columbus** [1451–1506] was a navigator, colonizer, and explorer whose voyages across the Atlantic Ocean led to general European awareness of the American continents. His initial 1492 voyage won the attention of Queen Isabella of Spain who was interested in discovering a more direct trade route to the lucrative Asian spice trade rather than trekking overland through Arabia.

**Amerigo Vespucci** [1454-1512], explorer and cartographer, verified that the New World discovered by Columbus in 1492 was not eastern Asia. The name "America," derived from the feminized Latin version of his first name, began being used on new 16th Century world maps. Other Italian explorers: **John Cabot**, who discovered Newfoundland and Labrador in Canada. **Giovanni da Verrezzano** was the first to explore the Atlantic coast and drop anchor in Manhattan in 1524.

**Machiavelli** [1469-1527], a diplomat and political philosopher. His surname has passed into common dialect, referring to any political move that is devious or cunning (i.e. Machiavellian).

**Maria Montessori** [1870-1952] was a physician, humanitarian, and devout Catholic. She is best known for her Montessori method of education of children from birth to adolescence.

**Galileo Galilei** [1564-1642] a mathematician and astronomer, who improved the telescope and astronomical observations. His contributions include the telescopic confirmation of the phases of Venus, the discovery of Jupiter's four largest satellites, and the observation of sunspots.

**Enrico Fermi** [1901-1954] was awarded the Nobel Prize in Physics in 1938 for his work on the development of the first nuclear reactor.

**Verdi** [1813-1901] was one of the most influential opera composers in the 19th Century. His *La Traviata*, *Aida*, *Rigoletto* dominate the standard repertoire 150 years after their composition.

**Toscanini** [1867-1954] is perhaps one of the greatest conductors of all time. After conducting at the Metropolitan Opera in New York, the NBC Symphony Orchestra was created for him in 1937.

**Guglielmo Marconi** [1874-1937] was best known for the development of a radiotelegraph system. He was awarded the 1909 Nobel Prize in Physics.

**Luigi Pirandello** [1867-1936] a novelist, awarded the Nobel Prize in Literature in 1934.

**Vittorio de Sica** [1901-1974] was a critically acclaimed actor and director. He was honored with 4 Academy Awards in the Best Foreign Film category. One of his best-received films was *Two Women*, starring Sophia Loren.

**Federico Fellini** [1920-1993] is considered one of the most influential and widely revered filmmakers of the 20th Century. His works garnered many international awards, including four Oscars.

**Sergio Leone** [1929-1989] directed the "spaghetti western" films: *A Fistful of Dollars*, *For a Few Dollars More*, *The Good, the Bad and the Ugly*, and *Once Upon a Time in the West*. He also turned down the opportunity to direct *The Godfather*.

**Franco Zeffirelli** [1923-] film director. He is also an opera director, designer and producer of opera, theatre, film, and television.

**Bernardo Bertolucci** [1940-] His 1987 film *The Last Emperor* won nine Oscars.

**Marcello Mastroianni** [1923-1996] was directed by Federico Fellini in *La Dolce Vita* and *8½*. He often co-starred with Sophia Loren.

**Sophia Loren** [1934-] born Sofia Villani Scicolone, won her first Academy Award for the 1961 film *Two Women*. Other actresses of note are **Anna Magnani, Gina Lollobrigida,** and **Isabella Rossellini.**

**Roberto Benigni** [1952-] starred in the international success *Life is Beautiful*, receiving three Academy Awards overall.

In Italian automobile design and manufacture of sports cars - **Ferruccio Lamborghini, Alfredino** and **Enzo Ferrari**, and **Nicola Romeo**.

*Clockwise: Christopher Columbus, Enrico Caruso, Luciano Pavarotti, Amerigo Vespucci and Michelangelo's* David *at center.*

In the world of fashion design, the most recognized are **Giorgio Armani, Fendi, Salvatore Ferragamo, Domenico Dolce** and **Stefano Gabbana, Guccio Gucci, Franco Moschino, Miuccia Prada, Nina Ricci, Elsa Schiaparelli, Donatella Versace,** and **Gianni Versace**.

There are many more Italians who have made this world a better place to live.

# Notable Italian Americans

*In spite of Italian passion and devotion to their mother country, the need to answer the call to America was greater. Italian immigrants made the arduous journey across a vast ocean for a variety of reasons, however, contrary to the age-old myths; they did not immigrate to America to seek streets paved with gold. They were much too intelligent to believe in that fairy tale. They came to seek the freedom to live, to work, to love, and perhaps most importantly to provide for future generations. Indeed, when they left their homes, their families, their friends, they certainly experienced the fears, anticipation, pain, and even a traumatic sense of both joy and sorrow.*

*Their ancestors came from all parts of Italy: Tuscany, Umbria, Veneto, Piedmont, Lombardy, Campania, Sicily, Abruzzi, Calabria, Bologna, Milano, and Naples. They were as diverse as the areas from which they came - their life's work, their dialects, and even their foods differed. Many followed their love of God, love of family, and their joy of living life to its fullest. Their courage was extraordinary. They asked nothing of anyone except that they be given work so that they might provide a better life for their families.*

*It is often unknown, less spoken of, or deliberately ignored that many intelligent, talented, brave Italians contributed to the growth of America in multiple diverse areas. Some of the names noted at right are easily recognized, however, some have been lost in history. It is imperative that we honor both.*

Some historians say that Italian-American recognition came strongly to the fore in the early 1980s: Paterno, Valvano, Massimino, Lasorda, Pacino, Stallone, Scorsese, Coppola, Iacocca, D'Amato, Domenici, DeNiro, Giamatti, and Rodino are a few of the names that testify to the cumulative achievement of Italian Americans.

**Henry Di Tonti,** known as "Tonti the Iron Hand" because he lost a hand in battle, accompanied Robert La Salle, a Frenchman, and explored for the first time the Great Lakes in *The Griffin*, a ship he built in 1679. Tonti also founded the first European settlement in Illinois in 1680, and the first French settlement in Arkansas in 1683. He sailed under the French flag because he was from Gaeta, near Rome, which was originally controlled by France. Today, Tontitown in Arkansas is named in his honor.

**Alphonse Di Tonti** was the co-founder of Detroit, Michigan in 1704 and its colonial governor for 12 years. He was the younger brother of explorer Henry Di Tonti.

**Colonel Francis Vigo** aided the American forces during the Revolutionary War and he was the foremost financier of the American Revolution in the Northwest. Vigo also helped to finance the George Rogers Clark expeditions. In 1800, he played an important role in opening the Northwest Territories for American settlement. Berra Park on the Hill was originally named Vigo Park.

The route to the source of the Mississippi River was discovered by **Giacomo Costantino Beltrami** while he was exploring the territory that later became Minnesota in 1823. In 1886, Minnesota created Beltrami County in honor of the explorer's discovery.

The words in the Declaration of Independence, "All men are created equal" were suggested to Thomas Jefferson by **Filippo Mazzei,** a Tuscan, Jefferson's friend and neighbor. Mazzei's original words were "All men are by nature equally free and independent."

Two of the original signers of the Declaration of Independence were of Italian origin: **William Paca** and **Caesar Rodney.** Paca was one of the first senators in the Maryland state legislature, governor of Maryland (1782 to 1785) and a major general during the Revolutionary War. Rodney of Delaware is most remembered for his courageous ride to Philadelphia in July 1776. Though sick with cancer, he rode through thunder and rain to arrive just in time to vote for independence.

**Giuseppe Garibaldi,** who led Italy to unification in 1861, was offered a command as Major General in the Union Army by President Lincoln. Garibaldi declined, but to honor him, the 39th New York Infantry was named the Garibaldi Guard. About 150 of its 850 men were Italian and fought in the Union Army from Bull Run to Appomattox.

**Attilio Piccirilli** and his five brothers, Neapolitan immigrants, carved the statue of Lincoln for the Lincoln Memorial — which they began in 1911 and completed in 1922. It is 19 feet high and made of 28 blocks of marble. He also carved the famous lions on the steps of the New York Public Library,

**Constantine Brumidi** in 1850 painted the historical frieze on the Capitol's Rotunda.

**Enrico Causici** sculpted relief panels on the United States Capitol.

**John Rapetti** worked in Paris with Frederic Bartholdi on the Statue of Liberty.

**John Palma** of Philadelphia gave the first concert on record in the colonies. Thomas Jefferson recruited **14 Italian musicians from Catania** to launch the U. S. Marine Corps Band.

**Over 300,000 Italian Americans,** including 87,000 Italian nationals, served in the U.S. military during World War I. Approximately 1.5 million Italian Americans served in World War II, "more than 10 percent of the might of the American forces in World War II."

**Rosie the Riveter,** who represented the millions of American women who took men's places in factories during World War II, was Rosie Bonavita of Long Island, New York

**Gov. Ella Tambussi Grasso** of Connecticut was the first American woman elected governor in her own right and the first Italian-American woman in Congress. Elected governor in 1975, she served in Congress from 1970 to 1974.

**Geraldine Ferraro** was the first woman to ever run for national office in the U.S. In 1984, she ran as Walter Mondale's vice presidential candidate.

**Mario Cuomo**, elected governor of New York in 1982, won the 1986 election with 2,761,000 votes, or 64 percent, the largest margin in New York history.

Brooklyn's **Rudolph W. Giuliani** was elected mayor of New York City in 1993, and re-elected in 1997. During his first term as mayor, crime in the Big Apple dropped 41 percent.

**Charles Joseph Bonaparte** founded the Federal Bureau of Investigation in 1908. He also built the U.S. Navy into one of the strongest in the world and was the first Italian American appointed to a cabinet position, serving as Secretary of the Navy and later as U.S. Attorney General during Theo-

dore Roosevelt's administration.

**Alfred E. Smith,** who was born Alfred Emanuele Ferrara, was the first Italian-American governor of New York (1919), and the first Italian-American presidential candidate.

**Frank Serpico** was a New York City undercover policeman whose exposure of police corruption led to the formation of the Knapp Commission. His life and work were the subject of a book by Peter Maas and a movie, starring Al Pacino.

**Antonin Scalia** is the first Italian American to serve on the U.S. Supreme Court. The son of Sicilian immigrants, he was appointed in 1986 by President Ronald Reagan.

**John Sirica** was the judge who presided over the Watergate case for 5 years. His decision led to President Nixon's resignation in 1974.

Known as "The Yankee Clipper," **Joseph Paul DiMaggio,** the son of Sicilian immigrants, had a 56-game hitting streak in 1941 which still stands as the longest in baseball history. He retired with 361 home runs, and 1,537 runs batted in. In 1950, Joe DiMaggio was voted the "Greatest Living Player" of baseball and in 1955, only four years after his retirement, he was inducted into the Baseball Hall of Fame.

**Yogi Berra** (See story in St. Louis Italians) led the Yankees to the American pennant, becoming the first Italian-American manager to win a league championship.

Known as "the Scooter" for his agility as a shortstop, **Phil Rizzuto** played for the Yankees from 1941 to 1954. A key member of the nine World Series classics, he had 200 hits in 1950 and was selected as the American League's most valuable player. After retiring, he became a sports announcer and was known as "the voice of the Yankees."

**Roy Campanella,** a catcher for the Brook-

*Geraldine Ferraro*

*Ernest and Julio Gallo*

lyn Dodgers, played in five World Series. He was named Most Valuable Player in 1951, 1953, and 1955. His career ended tragically when he was left paralyzed from a car crash.

Baseball's ambassador **Tommy Lasorda** in 1999 celebrated 50 years with the Dodgers. He holds the second longest tenure in baseball history with the same team. He led the Dodgers to a World Championship in 1981, three National League and five division titles. "Mr. Baseball" was named Manager of the Year four times, and managed in three World Series and three All-Star games.

**Billy Martin,** born Alfred Manuel Pesano, became the first Italian-American manager to win a World Series when he led the New York Yankees to victory in 1977. Four other Italian-American managers have led their teams to World Series victories: Tommy Lasorda led the Los Angeles Dodgers in 1981 and 1988, Joe Altobelli of the Baltimore Orioles in 1983, Tony LaRussa of the Oakland Athletics in 1989, and Joe Torre of the New York Yankees in 1996 and 1998.

**Buttercup Dickerson,** born Lewis Pessano in Tyaskin, Maryland in 1858, was the first Italian-American player in the major leagues. His first game was July 15, 1878 when he was the starting outfielder for Cincinnati.

Legendary football coach **Vince Lombardi** led the Green Bay Packers to five National Football League (NFL) championships (between 1959 and 1967), also winning the first and second Super Bowls (1967 and 1968). His motto was "Winning isn't everything. It's the only thing."

**Joe Paterno** became head coach of the Penn State football team in 1965 where he led the team to 22 major bowl games and four perfect seasons. 48 of his players joined the NFL. Three times honored as Coach of the Year, he won more than 80 percent of his games.

Seven Italian-American football players have won the Heisman Trophy. They are **Alan Ameche, Gary Beban, Joe Bellino, Angelo Bertelli, John Cappelletti, Gino Torretta, and Vinny Testaverde.**

The greatest Super Bowl drive of all time - eight complete passes in two minutes and thirty seconds was the work of San Francisco 49ers **Joe Montana** in 1984. Montana quarterbacked the 49ers to four Super Bowl titles before playing for the Kansas City Chiefs. He was the Most Valuable Player of three of those four Super Bowls.

**Dan Marino** played for the Miami Dolphins in 1984. He passed for an amazing 47 touchdowns in his first 20 games, a record it took Joe Namath three seasons to match.

**Brian Piccolo** was drafted by the Chicago Bears, with whom he gained 927 yards and caught 58 passes before his life was cut short by cancer in 1970 when he was 27 years old.

**Franco Harris,** a black Italian American whose mother came from Lucca, played for the Pittsburgh Steelers. He held the record for the most yards gained in a Super Bowl - 158 against the Minnesota Vikings in 1975.

**Rocky Marciano** was the heavyweight boxing champion of the world from 1952-1956 with a 49-0 record. His real name was Rocco Marchegiano. Middleweight boxing champions include; **Rocky Graziano** (1947); and **Jake LaMotta** (1949).

In hockey, brothers **Phil and Tony Esposito** have set records. Phil played for the Chicago Blackhawks, Boston Bruins and New York Rangers and was inducted into the Hockey Hall of Fame. He was general manager of the New York Rangers. **Tony Esposito** became one of the greatest goaltenders of all time with the Chicago Blackhawks. He was nicknamed "Tony O" for his 76 shutouts.

From 1986 to 1988, then-22-year-old Olympic champion **Brian Boitano** won the men's singles

*Enrico Fermi*

*Domenico Ghirardelli*

title at the annual World Figure Skating Championships. During the 1988 Olympics, he won the gold medal

In 1990, **Mary Lou Retton,** born Mary Lou Rettoni, became the first female gymnast and the youngest athlete ever inducted into the Olympic Hall of Fame. In the 1984 Olympics at age 16, she won the all-around gold medal in women's gymnastics.

**Charles Atlas,** born Angelo Siciliano, was dubbed "America's Most Perfectly Developed Man" by *Physical Culture* magazine. By the 1950s, the former Coney Island janitor, had over one million adherents.

When Prohibition was lifted in 1933, brothers **Ernest and Julio Gallo** took their entire savings, $5,000, to produce wine from their father's vineyards in California. This helped to launch California's wine industry. Today more than 100 wineries in the U.S. are owned by Italian Americans.

Prince Company, a $200 million-a-year pasta manufacturing business, was established by **Joseph Pellegrino,** who immigrated to the U.S. from Sicily at age 12. A former street hustler, Pellegrino only went to school through the eighth grade.

**Lee Iacocca,** born "Lido", brought the Chrysler Corporation back from the brink of bankruptcy during the mid-1980s. The company was in the black within a month of his tenure as chairman.

The Jacuzzi hot tub and spa were invented by the **Jacuzzis,** whose family came to America in 1907. They also supplied the American military with propellers.

The chocolate bar exists today in part thanks to **Domenico Ghirardelli.** In 1867, he perfected a method to make ground chocolate. Ghirardelli chocolate is sold all over the world, including in the square in San Francisco named after him.

**Richard A. Grasso** was elected chairman and chief executive officer of the New York Stock Exchange in 1995. He started at the Exchange in 1968 and steadily rose through the ranks.

The man who put a hand-held hair dryer in every beauty salon and American home is **Leandro ("Lee") Rizzuto,** chairman and president of Conair Corporation of Connecticut. The company was founded in 1959 with $100 and its invention of hot rollers. In 1971, Conair perfected the professional pistol-grip hair dryer. Rizzuto also owns Cuisinart.

Tropicana was founded in 1947 by **Anthony Rossi** as a Florida fruit packaging company. In 1954, Rossi pioneered a pasteurization process for orange juice. Today owned by PepsiCo.,Tropicana is the world's largest producer of fruit juices.

The ice cream cone was invented in 1896 by **Italo Marcioni** in New Jersey. Two generations later in Pittsburgh, McDonald's franchise owner, Jim Delligatti, invented the Big Mac.

The suburban shopping mall was developed by **William Cafaro** and **Edward J. DeBartolo.** Cafaro pioneered the enclosed American Mall in Lima, Ohio in 1965. DeBartolo built the first American shopping plaza in the 1940s.

**Mother Frances Cabrini,** the first American saint, founded 14 American colleges, 98 schools, 28 orphanages, 8 hospitals, and 3 training schools with the help of over 4,000 sisters she recruited for the Missionary Sisters of the Sacred Heart. Mother Cabrini immigrated to the U.S. in 1889 and was canonized in 1949.

In 1950, **Dr. Margaret J. Giannini** founded the Mental Retardation Institute in New York City, the first and largest facility for the mentally handicapped in the world.

**Gay Talese** was a prolific writer, and a reporter for *The New York Times* between 1956 and 1965, writing about sports and politics. Among his many bestsellers is *Unto the Sons,* a largely autobiographi-

*Rudolph Valentino*

*Charles Atlas*

11

cal book about his Italian heritage.

**Robert De Niro** has paintings in the Metropolitan and Brooklyn Museums and other major institutions. He is the father of the famous film actor who bears his name.

Artist **Georgia O'Keeffe** was of Italian descent. Her mother was Ida Totto and the artist was named for her maternal grandfather, Giorgio Totto.

**Gian Carlo Menotti** composed *Amahl and the Night Visitors* (1951) and *The Saint of Bleeker Street* (1955), an opera set in a modern Little Italy. His operas *The Consul* and *The Saint of Bleeker Street* won him Pulitzer Prizes.

The Metropolitan Opera became one of the finest opera companies in the world under the legendary leadership of its manager, **Giulio Gatti-Casazza** (1869-1940) who brought to its stage a brilliant array of singers, including **Enrico Caruso** and **Enzio Pinza** as well as the conductor **Arturo Toscanini.** Gatti-Casazza managed the Met from 1908 to 1935.

One of Hollywood's most gifted directors, **Frank Capra** was born in Sicily in 1897, and spent his sixth birthday in steerage on a 13-day ocean voyage to America. He is perhaps most famous for his film *It's a Wonderful Life*, but his film portfolio includes *It Happened One Night* (1934) with Clark Gable, and *Mr. Smith Goes to Washington* (1939), starring Jimmy Stewart. Capra won three Academy Awards for Best Director.

Among the many Italian Americans in Hollywood is the legendary father-and-son team of **Carmine and Francis Ford Coppola,** who won four Oscars in 1975 for The Godfather, Part II. Carmine, who was a flautist for Arturo Toscanini, composed the soundtrack and Francis, who first won an Oscar for *Patton*, directed the film.

The producer of all but one of the first 17 James Bond movies was **Albert R. "Cubby" Broccoli**. Broccoli launched the 007 film series in 1962 with *Dr. No*. His ancestors invented broccoli by-crossing cauliflower seeds with pea seeds in Italy in the 19th Century.

**Louis Prima** was a trumpeter, composer, and band leader. His greatest achievement was his 1936 composition *Sing, Sing, Sing* which was later recorded by Benny Goodman.

**Harry Warren** was born Salvatore Guaragna in Brooklyn and was the son of a Calabrian bootmaker. One of Hollywood's most successful composers, he wrote *Chattanooga Choo Choo, I Only Have Eyes For You*, and *That's Amore*. Between 1935 and 1950, he wrote more hit songs than Cole Porter, Irving Berlin or George Gershwin, three of which earned him Academy Awards: *Lullaby of Broadway, You'll Never Know*, and *Atchison Topeka and Santa Fe.*

Four-time Academy Award and 20-time Grammy and Gold Record winner **Henry Mancini** is remembered for his classic *Moon River* from *Breakfast at Tiffany's*. He also wrote the scores for 80 other movies. His break came when he scored the theme music to *Peter Gunn*, a popular TV series of the early 1960s.

Conductor and composer **Bill Conti** wrote the theme song, *Gonna Fly Now* to the classic movie *Rocky* in 1976. He has since scored more than 70 movies. He composed for *The Right Stuff*, for which he received an Academy Award in 1983.

Born Alfred Cucozza in Philadelphia in 1921, **Mario Lanza** took his mother's name as his stage name and became the first vocalist to sell 2.5 million albums, making 390 records. An embolism struck him down in Rome at age 38 in 1959.

**Frank Sinatra,** the Oscar, Emmy, and Grammy-winning legend known as "The Chairman of the Board," was born in Hoboken, New Jersey in

*Jimmy Durante*

*Penny Marshall*

1915. He made more than 2,000 recordings and raised millions of dollars for charities during his 60-year career.

Among the many Italian Americans who popularized American songs here and abroad are **Vic Damone (Vito Farinola); Dean Martin (Dino Crocetti); Tony Bennett (Anthony Benedetto); Frankie Laine (Frank Lo Vecchio); Perry Como, Frankie Avalon (Frank Avalone); Bobby Rydell (Roberto Ridarelli); Connie Francis (Concetta Franconero); Bobby Darin (Walden Cassotto);** and **Jon Bon Jovi.** Rock star **Madonna** was born **Louise Veronica Ciccone. Bruce Springsteen's** mother was Adele Ann Zerilli.

**Rudolph Valentino** was an actor, sex symbol, and early pop icon. Known as the "Latin Lover," he was one of the most popular stars of the 1920s, and one of the most recognized stars from the silent movie era. Some of his best known roles include the silent films *The Sheik* and *The Four Horsemen of the Apocalypse.* His untimely death at age 31 caused mass hysteria among his female fans, propelling him into icon status.

Vaudeville legend and early television star **Jimmy Durante,** born in New York City in 1893, insured his enormous nose, which he called his "schnozzola," for a million dollars. During the 1940s, this Emmy-winner's radio program was a Friday night fixture.

With a pregnant wife and only $100 in the bank, **Sylvester Stallone**, the Italian Stallion, wrote the script for *Rocky* in three and a half days. Stallone, age 30, refused to sign the contract unless he played the lead. He is one of the highest-paid actors of all time.

Entertainers **Susan Sarandon** and **Anne Bancroft [Anna Maria Louisa Italiano]** are Italian American.

**Penny Marshall (Carole Penny Masciarelli)** has made a remarkable transition from star of the hit TV series *Laverne & Shirley* to one of the few women directors in Hollywood.

Hollywood has a large number of actors of Italian descent who have maintained their ethnic identity and achieved stardom despite having names that are not easily spelled or pronounced. These actors light up the marquee with their ethnicity: **Robert De Niro**, **Al Pacino**, **John Travolta**, **Leonardo DiCaprio**, **Danny DeVito**, **Joe Mantegna**, **Dennis Farina**, **Scott Baio**, **Susan Lucci**, **Annette Funicello**, **James Gandolfini**, **Sonny Bono**, **Ray Liotta**, **Joe Pesci**, **Ben Gazzara**, **Tony Franciosa**, **Danny Aiello,** and **Paul Giamatti.**.

Many Italian-American actors changed the family surname often on the advice of their agents. **Connie Stevens** was born **Concetta Rosalie Ingolia**, **Robert Blake** was born **Michael Gubitosi**, **Nicholas Cage** was born **Nicholas Coppola**, **Vince Edwards** was born **Vincent Zoino**, **Talia Shire** was born **Talia Coppola**, **James Darren** was born **James Ercolani**, and **Tony Danza** was born **Anthony Iadanza**.

The man behind Tom and Jerry, Yogi Bear, The Flintstones, The Jetsons, The Smurfs, and Scooby-Doo is **Joseph Barbera**, co-founder of Hanna-Barbera Film Studios. He met Bill Hanna in 1937. In 1957, they started their own animation studio and went on to win seven Oscars.

Italian-American cartoonists have created some of the world's most popular animated characters including: Donald Duck, created by **Alfred Tagliafero**; Woody Woodpecker, a creation of **Walter Lantz** (born "Lanza"); and Casper the Friendly Ghost, the brainchild of **Joseph Oriolo.**

*Perry Como*

*Frank Sinatra*

# Notable St. Louis Italians

It is well to recognize that celebrities of today make news but heroes are people who make history. Pictured are notable Italian St. Louisans whose names have stood the test of time. We have only to follow the thread of our local heritage to find the great Italian men and women who are dear to St. Louis. Each profile begins with the individual's birthplace in Italy and the year they came to America.

Information used from the book *The Italians in Missouri* (1929) by Giovanni Schiavo.

Victor Berlendis–Venice–1893–one of the leading architectural sculptors (of models made of clay, wood, and marble) in the country–sought after by leading institutions and universities for his work.

Vincent Borghesi–Bagni di Lucca–1906–President, Roman Art Company (marble statues, fine wrought iron products, and electrical fixtures)–resided on the Hill.

Guglielmo Cataldi–Palermo–1905–Physician and Surgeon–was a Captain in the Italian Medical Reserve Corps–Owner of Rome Pharmacy on 7th Street–freely offered time and money for the advancement of St. Louis Italians.

Paul Calcaterra–Detroit, Michigan–Funeral Director–owned several local funeral parlors–took an active interest in Italian affairs by joining Italian fraternal organizations and societies.

Angelo Corrubia–Potenza–1902–Architect with degrees from Washington University (where he later designed campus buildings) and M.I.T.–designed the Catholic Church of St. Ambrose which is central to the Hill's society.

Humberto Ghio–St. Louis, Missouri–Dentist who attended medical school at St. Louis University–One of the founders of the Italian Fraternal & Investment Bldg.–a member of one of the oldest and most famous Italian families in St. Louis.

Isidoro Oldani–Milan–1902–President, Blue Ridge Bottling Company which eventually produced 140,000 cases of mineral water each year. A resident of the Hill, he was active in the Knights of Columbus.

14

Benjamin Garavelli–Bassignana–1895–Restaurateur–After working at the Waldorf Astoria in New York, his nightclub would be one of the best in St. Louis where epicureans could find the food of their choice.

Joseph Garavelli–Bassignana–1903–Highly regarded owner of Garavelli's Restaurant, once the most popular restaurant in St. Louis. Did more than anyone to introduce Italians as important additions to the City of St. Louis.

John Ravarino–Bassignana–1898–Vice President, Ravarino & Freschi Importing and Mfg. Co. The Italian government bestowed on him and his partner, Joseph Freschi, the Cross of the Italian Crown in 1929.

Joseph Freschi–Bassignana–1890–President, Ravarino & Freschi Importing & Mfg. Co.(importing business and macaroni plant)–Philanthropist active in the affairs of the Italian community.

Vito Viviano–Terrasini–1900–President, Viviano & Bros. Macaroni Mfg. Co., one of the largest in the country–later added a grocery department and bakery–the Italian government bestowed on him the Cross of the Crown for his philanthropy.

Ignazio Riggio–Palermo–1900–President, Riggio Realty Company–Undoubtably, the most popular person on the Hill where he had acquired the trust of both Northern and Southern Italians due to his moral and commercial integrity.

John Volpi–Milan–1900–Owner, Volpi Packing Company which produced superior quality salami in the Italian style. One of the leading Italians on the Hill, he never missed an opportunity to help St. Ambrose Church.

Mariano Balsamo–Termini Imerese–1894–President, Fruit Supply Co., the largest wholesale fruit company in St. Louis. Balsamo also owned 1,800 acres of land in Texas.

# "It Ain't Over Till Its Over" – Yogi Berra

Someone once said that the worst times make the best people. If that is the case, then Yogi Berra was one of the best. But it was not only bad times that made the man – he was the best at his best. And the Hill in St. Louis witnessed those life and times.

Casey Stengel, manager of the New York Yankees, once said, "Yogi could fall in a sewer and come up with a gold watch." Not quite true because this man knew something more durable than luck: a strong, supportive and loving family life.

His neighborhood was the Hill, the Italian section in southwest St. Louis, a place where most everyone was from the Old Country, still spoke the language and carried on the tradition as if no ocean was crossed, no hurdles to leap over. After his birth, his family moved from Columbus Avenue to Elizabeth Avenue. Right

across the street lived his best buddy, Joe Garagiola, whose father worked with his father at the Laclede-Christy Clay Products Company.

There on the Hill, you were what you were; everyone took care of each other, worked hard, tended their small, neat bungalows and, as time passed, handed them down to the next generation. But during the times of Yogi in the 1930s, life was tough. At the brick kilns, his papa worked in a sweatbox and when he wasn't doing that, he was bricklaying. He used to point at the St. Louis Arena when they passed it by and remind the family that he helped "support" and build the place. Yogi's parents considered baseball something you played, like bocce, an enjoyable pastime on the way to better things – like bricklaying. When the 4:30 factory whistle blew, Yogi had to stop playing ball, collect fifteen cents from his mother, run

to Fassi's and pick up a tureen of beer, for when his father got home. Though his father felt that this discipline might deter him from his game, it had the opposite effect.

As Yogi remembers, "I must have been ten or eleven when I began to play ball. All the kids around my age who lived on Elizabeth Avenue made up a sports club called the Stags, and we played in the street, in the Shaw School yard, two blocks away and in Sublette Park, half a mile away. We even built ourselves the 1936 equivalent of a little league ball park on the Clay Mine, the neighborhood garbage dump that's been all filled in and has a street on it now called Berra Court. Grabbing some flour, the gang made base lines, dug a big hole, and pushed an old junky car inside. That was the dugout." Yogi was soon ready for the big time. But first he had to get by papa.

*Many great names in one photograph: At left, Joe Garagiola, baseball; Lou Thesz, wrestler; Sam Muchnick, promoter; Joe Louis, boxer; Stan Musial, baseball; Yogi Berra, baseball; and Red Schoendienst, baseball.*

Wanting to play ball, Yogi luckily had his brothers on his side. His father was convinced he'd land up a bum on the street, but his siblings pleaded to let him have the chance they never got.

In 1942, both Yogi and Joe Garagiola tried out for the St. Louis Cardinals; eager, excited and determined to do their best, not only for themselves but for their families and friends on the Hill. Both were catchers and left-handed hitters but somehow Joe was the one who caught their professional eye. Branch Rickey, the general manager gave him a $500 signing bonus but Yogi got nothing.

However, a knock on his door saved the day. Johnny Schulte heard about "Lawdy" from his friend, Leo Brown, head of the American Legion team. Brown had told him that Yogi was worth the same signing bonus. Brown agreed and signed him up with the $500 bonus and a salary of $90 a month to play for the Norfolk Virginia Class B Piedmont League. On September 22, 1946, Yogi walked into Yankee stadium for the first time.

Many people wonder how this baseball great got his nickname. According to Mickey Garagiola, Joe's brother, it was a Yankee teammate that gave Lawrence the nickname "Yogi" in the 1940s because Lawdy used to sit in the dugout with arms folded and legs crossed, resembling a yogi.

Regardless, Yogi determined to never embarrass himself on the field. He belonged in the game and it was imperative that his family and friends on the Hill knew this. There was one person, though, who saw past the homely face and short, bullish build.

As Joe Garagiola related, "…Yogi always wanted to go to Musial and Biggie's for lunch.

*Yogi enjoys time with his niece, Diana Berra Pozzo.*

We couldn't afford to eat there, so we just sat. Finally I figured out that he just wanted to look at this waitress, Carmen [Short]. He kept saying, 'She won't go out with me.' I'd say, 'Ask her, Yogi.' He did. She married him." They were wed in the same church as his parents on the corner of Marconi and Wilson, on the Hill. They produced three sons and ten grandchildren. Initially, even though he had played in a World Series, Yogi and Carmen moved in with his parents on Elizabeth during the off-season and Yogi worked for Ruggeri's Restaurant, greeting customers and handing out a card indicating his World Series participation. Yogi was always a dependable Ruggeri's worker "except when there was a hockey game."

Though this great man may be remembered as the one who "got away" from the Hill, Yogi Berra will always remain in the hearts of St. Louisans as the kid on Elizabeth Avenue squinting at the sun as he caught a great fly ball, dragging beer home from the saloon for his hard-working father or daydreaming in his classroom at Shaw Grammar School that one day he'd make everyone on the Hill proud. Did he? The answer to that is way out of the ballpark.

## YOGIISMS

"We made too many wrong mistakes."

"If people don't want to come to the ballpark, how are you going to stop them?"

"If I didn't wake up I'd still be sleeping."

"I usually take a two-hour nap from 1 to 4."

"We have a good time together, even when we're not together."

"Little League baseball is a good thing 'cause it keeps the parents off the streets and the kids out of the house!"

When asked by a reporter if Joe DiMaggio was fast, he answered: "No, he just got there in time."

During an interview, Arlene Francis asked Yogi if he had read the new book, *Yogi: It Ain't Over…* Yogi answered: "No, I was there."

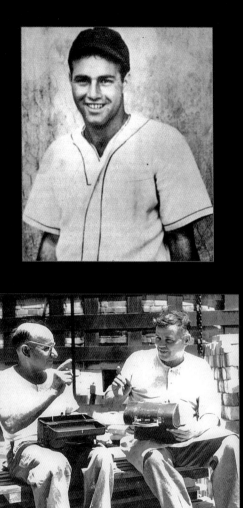

*Yogi Berra's father, Peter, at left, and Joe Garagiola's father, "Big John," take a lunch break at Laclede-Christy mine. It was here that Mickey and Joe Garagiola came when Joe was 15 (photo above) with a $500 signing bonus from the Cardinals to get Papa's signature and okay, as Joe was still a minor. The $500 bonus paid off the Garagiola home mortgage, so John signed.*

# JOE GARAGIOLA

If there ever was a man who never strayed far from his roots, Joe Garagiola is the guy. Maybe it's because that is where the wellspring of his past lies. Down deep below the rich soil of the Hill you can find what fed and nurtured his illustrious career that spanned many decades: his family, his religion, and his friendships.

"My Pop came to America in 1911 from Inveruno, Italy, with a sign around his neck that read, 'St. Louis.' It was several years before he could send for Momma. Meanwhile he worked as a laborer who didn't speak any English, which was a barrier that had a powerful effect on his life. It forced him to go to work when he was sick, though he should have stayed home. He was afraid he'd be fired if he didn't show up and afraid he wouldn't be able to get another job because he didn't speak English. But my father did speak two languages, though: Italian and straightforward." Just like our Joe.

Joe was born on Sublette Avenue on February 12th, 1926 and grew up at 5446 Elizabeth Avenue, just across the street from another straight-talking baseball great, Yogi Berra. Their friendship on the Hill strengthened their ties through the years, but it was also Joe's respect for his friend's abilities that won him over. He once joked, "Not only was I *not* the best catcher in the Major Leagues, I wasn't even the best catcher on my block."

Raised in a Catholic family, religion played a large role in Garagiola's life. However, being an energetic growing boy with a mischievous streak, he couldn't resist tampering with the Testament. Once, while trying to get a laugh out of one of the nuns in religion class, he was asked, "What was St. Paul's vision on the way to Damascus?" and his quick answer was, "20/20." However, many of life's important lessons he learned along the way can be attributed to the nuns and priests who taught and disciplined him. His good penmanship goes all the way back to his days at St. Ambrose – great for signing those baseballs.

Joe's talents became too obvious to miss by the time he was 15 years old. Asked to try out for the Cardinals by their scout, Dee Walsh, he was short on shoes and a baseball glove. But the network on the Hill took care of matters in quick succession. As he tells it, "Monk Berra [no relation to Yogi], had the only pair of baseball shoes and they were size 10C. But by stuffing the front with rags and cotton, you could make 5's out of them. The catcher's mitt was the problem. None of the guys had one. The only one we know of belonged to Louie Cassani. He wasn't one of the boys, but Father Palumbo said that our Johnny Colombo knew Gino Pariani who knew Louie Cassani. The network began the operation and they got the mitt for me."

Signed at 15 by Branch Rickey, Garagiola played for the Cardinals for five seasons, including the 1946 championship year. The first World Series Joe ever saw was the one that he played in as a rookie catcher, just home from the war. He hit .316 in the series and batted in four runs in one game. After the Cardinals, Garagiola played for the Pittsburgh Pirates and the Chicago Cubs. For nine years he was a journeyman catcher in the National League, tallying 42 home runs and a lifetime average of .257.

After his pro career ended in 1954, he joined St. Louis radio station KMOX and broadcast Cardinals games the next year. Once he moved to the Yankees, he called baseball for NBC for almost 30 years. He began doing national baseball broadcasts for NBC in 1961 and also called some World Series games on NBC Radio. After a stint doing New York Yankees games from 1965 to 1967, he was on board to call Mickey Mantle's 500th home run. He returned to broadcasting NBC baseball in 1974.

This baseball player moved from being a team player, to a broadcaster to media star to presidential pal. He co-hosted with Barbara Walters the early morning *Today Show* and acted as a guest host for Johnny Carson on the *Tonight Show*, including a live appearance of Beatles Paul McCartney and John Lennon. The *Tonight Show* highlighted Garagiola's quick wit and mischievous ways learned from his school days on the Hill which matched that of Johnny Carson himself. But according to his brother, Mickey, "Living in Scarsdale, New York and traveling in and out of the NBC broadcasting station everyday for two to three days every week got to be an exhausting challenge for my brother."

While working on a series of television ads for Gerald Ford, he and the president-to-be became fast friends. On election night, Ford invited Garagiola to be one of his guests at the White House to watch the election results.

Though this man was inducted in the Broadcaster's Wing of the National Baseball Hall of Fame in 1991 and has his own star on the St. Louis Walk of Fame, he has humbly considered that what baseball has given to him, he would return in aces. He chaired a

committee that has helped former professional baseball players and family who had fallen on hard times. Certainly he knew what that's all about, having to borrow a glove and stuff someone else's shoes to audition for the big time. However, he was coming from a place called the Hill where family is everything and friends are really something.

It seems when it came to romance, Joe never looked beyond the ball park. He met a young lady who later worked as an organist atop the ballpark at Busch Stadium. She hailed from St. Louis and her name was Audrie Ross. In 1949, she became his wife and together they raised three children, one of whom, Joe, Jr., became the general manager of the Arizona Diamondbacks.

After Joseph Garagiola attained some fame, a story goes that he did not forget his St. Ambrose and South Side Catholic classmates, nor his friends from the old neighborhood. Vincent DiRaimondo recalled Garagiola during World War II. DiRaimondo was stationed in the Philippines and heard that Joe was playing baseball in Manilla. In fact, Joe was the captain of that team. When DiRaimondo called out, "Hey Joe, I'm from the Hill." Immediately, Joe turned around and had him escorted to the dugout. DiRaimondo said, "Guess what, half the dugout was filled with guys from the Hill."

After his retirement from baseball, Garagiola lent his name to a 1960 book, first of three titles, *Baseball is a Funny Game,* which sold very well when it was released and established him as a "personality."

But, you know, that was no surprise to his family, his friends, the nuns and priests on the Hill because they already knew that.

*Pictured in 1941 with "Big John," their father, at photo left is Mickey Garagiola, longtime Ruggeri's waiter and wrestling announcer, with his brother, baseball great, NBC announcer and TV host Joe Garagiola. Even back then, Mickey had more hair than Joe.*

*In 1991, on the occasion of Joe Garagiola's induction in the Baseball Hall of Fame, Broadcaster's Wing, brother Mickey Garagiola gets in the action and is photographed with baseball greats, left to right, Willie McCovey, Ernie Banks, Mickey, Bill White (President of the National League), and Willie Mays.*

# TOM LOMBARDO

Perhaps learning from his father Angelo's dedication to family and work, Tom Lombardo developed his natural athletic and leadership abilities to amazing ends. From his freshman year at Soldan High School, Tom Lombardo was the football star of the city, garnering selection to the All-City and All-District Teams time and again, and was awarded the title of Most Valuable Player in his senior year.

Though courted by colleges around the nation, Tom chose to attend Saint Louis University, where he continued to play stellar football. He might have stayed there had it not been for the Japanese attack on Pearl Harbor on December 7, 1941. However, the events of that day stirred the fierce patriotism in the heart of this first-generation American, and as a result, Tom transferred to West Point.

At West Point, Tom reached unfathomable athletic heights when in 1944, as captain, he led the greatest football team in the history of that military academy. Indeed, Tom's team not only won the national championship; they had a perfect season, scoring an unbelievable 504 points to their opponents' 35. The squad featured two running backs many consider the greatest offensive tandem ever; Mr. Inside - Felix "Doc" Blanchard and Mr. Outside - Glenn Davis.

Lt. Thomas Lombardo called upon those exceptional leadership skills in the Korean War, when he led his regiment to take a hill from enemy forces near Ch'ogye, Korea, on September 24, 1950. Tragically, Tom was struck down by enemy fire as the enemy retreated.

Tom received many accolades following his death, including one by General Douglas MacArthur, who dedicated a field in Tom's honor in Seoul, South Korea. Moreover, the St. Louis branch of the National Football Foundation is named in honor of this great athlete and American hero. However, the most poignant praise still comes from his family. Though it has been almost 58 years since they lost their brother too soon, Carmen, Angelo, Jr., and Gus, owners of Lombardo's Restaurant, still beam with pride at the mention of his name.

The loss of Tom was a terrible blow to the Lombardo Restaurant family, yet they carried on admirably, working hard to not only keep the family going strong, but to continue delivering the same level of excellent service to their customers and community.

*With Davis and Blanchard, Army went 27-0-1 between 1944 and 1946. Tom (third from left in photo at right) captained the undefeated 1944 squad which outscored their opponents 504-35. Blanchard won the Heisman Trophy in 1945; Davis won in 1946. Davis scored a then-record 59 touchdowns; Blanchard scored 38. Davis still holds the all-time record for most yards averaged per carry in a season, with 11.5 yards in 1945.*

**Ernest Trova,** born in St. Louis on February 19, 1927, became one of the significant artists of the late twentieth century. Trova's gift of forty of his works led to the opening of St. Louis County Laumeier Sculpture Park. With his Falling Man (shown above), Ernest Trova created one of the defining artistic images of his time. Ernest Tino Trova, an American sculptor and painter, was a self-taught artist. He did not believe in taking art lessons. In 1944, he began to draw and paint in watercolors. In 1946, he produced his first casein and latex pictures. Following this, he began to experiment with a variety of media, often incorporating printed words, and also produced collages, assemblages, and sculptures. He had his first one-man show in 1959 at the Image Gallery in St. Louis.

Trova considered his entire output a single "work in progress." He lives in Richmond Heights, Missouri. Trova was inducted into the St. Louis Walk of Fame on May 17th, 1992, in the field of Art/Architecture. The location of his star is 6335 Delmar.

Until his death in 1964 **Lou "Midge" Berra** devoted his life to Hill politics. "I remember a variety of visitors," recalled Lou Berra, Jr., Midge's son, who, in 1973, served as assistant to Mayor John Poelker and now serves in Urban Affairs: "My parent's house was like Grand Central Station. Any time of the morning or evening, people would come and go needing favors from my Dad. My Dad spent countless hours at the police station, straightening out kids and getting them out of trouble. Police would call my Dad first then their parents. That's why he was called 'The King of the Hill.' He helped everyone. The elderly immigrants used to call him President Berra."

Skif is the perfect name for **Nina Ganci's** avant-garde clothing company. Skif, short for "schifo," is an Italian term used in Milan to describe the way she spoke Italian. According to Nina, her Italian was truly "fractured" since it was a combination of the Sicilian dialect she learned in Belgium and the Sicilian dialect she picked up in America. The term skif also carried over into her "irregular" or different designs. (A model, at right, wears one of Nina's sweaters.) Skif also provided an acronym which represents her personal philosophy as it translates into "Sweaters Knitted In Freedom."

Nina Ganci grew up in Liege, Belgium. Her parents, Dora and Pasquale Ganci, immigrated and settled in St. Louis. Nina attended New York's Fashion Institute before spending a year in Milan learning business skills from Antonio Guidoni. But in Nina's heart, she truly wanted to be as free and loose in her designs as she was in her language. She studied design in Paris under the renowned designer, Margiela. Upon returning to the United States in 1994, she settled in St. Louis to start her own business on Washington Avenue. In 2002, she purchased the Spielberg Furniture Building on the Hill at Daggett and Marconi.

Nina Ganci, the daughter of Italian immigrants, certainly has come a long way from the work her mother endured when she worked locally at Miss Elaine's Bridal Gown Company. Her job was to meticulously sew lace into the bodice of the bride's gown for a mere 18 cents a piece.

When Nina was asked the impetus that made her company succeed, she replied, "Having an Italian mother and father who gave me unconditional love and an understanding between right and wrong. They also stressed a love for God and self-respect."

The Hill community is fortunate and proud to see this young lady, with that pixie smile of hers, become nationally successful. Nina Ganci returns that affection, affirming, "I love the Hill. This is our home."

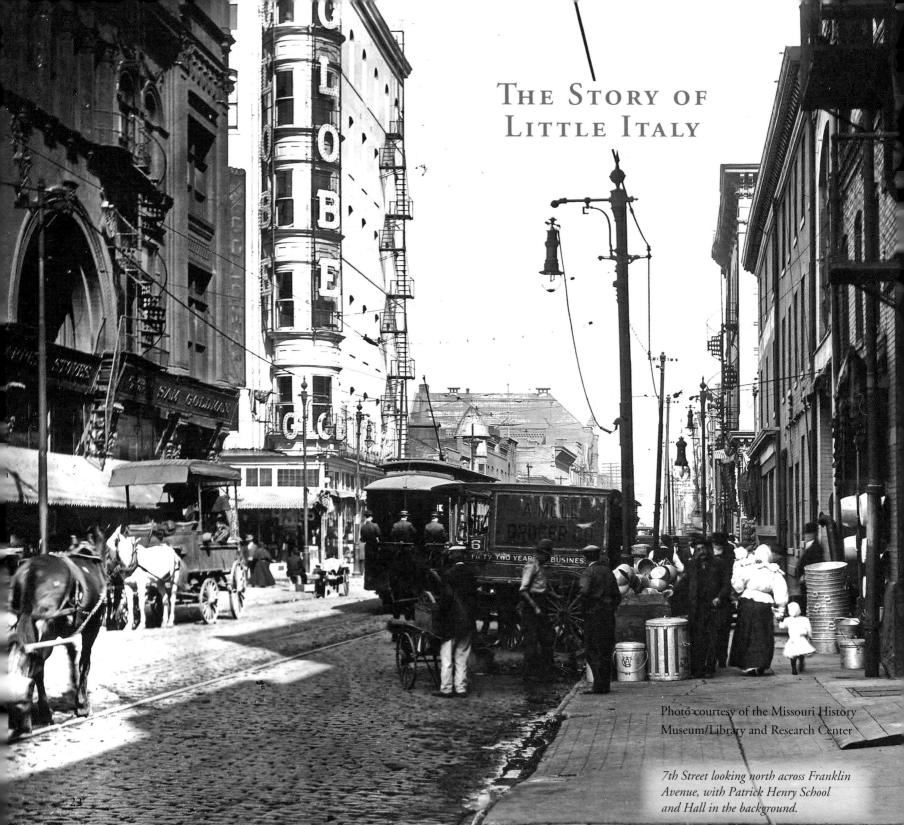

# THE STORY OF LITTLE ITALY

Photo courtesy of the Missouri History Museum/Library and Research Center

*7th Street looking north across Franklin Avenue, with Patrick Henry School and Hall in the background.*

## Little Italy: The Early Years

Excerpt from the *75ᵗʰ Anniversary of the Fratellanza* (1941) booklet. — "The City of St. Louis, which was founded in 1764 by Auguste Chouteau and thirty French pioneers, has had an unusual and remarkable progress since these first adventurers established a fur trading post here. Situated on the banks of the Mississippi River and forming the gateway to the far West, it grew and expanded until the year 1866. In the beginning, we find it to be a fairly large city with a population of 275,464 and ranking fourteenth in the country. The Civil War had more or less temporarily halted the remarkable growth of the city. In 1866, we find St. Louis gradually resuming the giant strides of its early history and here we discover the Italian immigrant doing his or her part for its progress. Although some Italians had ventured as far west as St. Louis in 1780, the first actual settlement of

Italians did not occur until 1848 when the official directory of that time shows that about 50 Italians resided here. And those few came, for the most part, from the northern part of Italy. Despite the fact that the first St. Louis bishop, Joseph Rosati, had been appointed to this area in 1827, in 1866 there were no less than 600 Italians living in St. Louis, 75 percent of these men were from small Appenine villages in the province of Genoa. All of these lived within a stone's throw of one another–from the levee to Twelfth Street, from Franklin Avenue to Spruce Street. Some of these Italians hired themselves out to "railroad bosses" and assisted in the building of the West. Most of them, however, started small businesses, such as fruit merchants, grocers, saloons, barber shops, confectioneries, etc., while not a few drifted into the fur business. The directory of that year also shows two Italian doctors, a lawyer and a teacher; so all in all, these Italians were more or less fairly represented in all businesses, industries, and professions. Their homes, too, were more or less multiple dwellings, that is, two- or three-story buildings in which three or more families were divided into various sections on each floor, with normal conveniences of that period since illumination was mostly by coal oil lamps. The electric light bulb was not as yet invented by Edison. Water had to be purified before it was fit to drink. This was usually done by filling huge barrels with water and placing alum therein. The old family washtub became the bathtub, since the comforts of the present lavatories had not as yet come into vogue, and yet all these homes were strongly built, for it was the Iron Age, with huge pillars of decorative iron which served to hold the high-ceilinged floors of brick and masonry.

*Photo Above: In 1960, Angelina Tinervia barbecues in one of the tenement backyards in Little Italy. Photo Below: In the mid-1950s, a pleasant sidewalk conversation between, left to right, Mr. Cierdo, Mr. Mache, and Mr. Massarro in Little Italy. Photo Left: Best friends in Little Italy.*

23

Transportation was by horse and buggy and the horse-drawn team, since nearly all streets were narrow and made of solid cobblestones while the sidewalks were of brick. Even streetcars were pulled by horses.

These Italians amused themselves as best they knew how. The bocce game was one of the outdoor diversions of the men, however, there were the usual dances, picnics, parties and theaters, which were more popular than our movies of today since there were no radios, automobiles and baseball games to interfere with these indoor amusements. The city limits were not much farther west than Jefferson Avenue. Italians were among the last of European races to come to the New World in appreciable numbers. They came from the numerous provinces which represented all parts of the Italian peninsula. The Southern Italians, from Sicily and Sardinia, represented the Mediterannean race in which Greek, Spanish, Saracen, and even African blood is fused."

## Little Italy

Between the years 1890 and 1930, Italians from Sicily immigrated to the United States in appreciable numbers. They came to seek a better life for their children—to escape living in dire poverty, to find freedom from the oppression of *padrones* (bosses), and, later, to escape the cruelty of the Fascists.

They arrived with the bare essentials of life as well as being unable to speak the language. They came with little money and no assurance of finding work, but possessed a spirit of determination and courage. They also came with their name on badges, attached on Ellis Island. The latter denied access to anyone setting foot onto American soil unless the immigrants could prove that a close relative was able to sponsor and support them. As the Sicilian

*Father Cesare Spigardi (photo inset left) in 1900 established, for the benefit of Little Italy, Our Lady Help of Christians (photo inset right, exterior) mission church. The church interior is pictured below.*

24

and Calabrian dialect was very different from the Lombardy, or Northern-Italian spoken on the Hill, the Sicilians tended to congregate in the near north side which was at 7th and Carr. The towns they came from were Cinisi, Terrasini, Marsala, Mazzara, and Campobello in Sicily. They had been predominantly people of the soil. But in America they had to accept any work they could find–from clay mining to street cleaning to streetcar track-work, and shoe repairing. Life was not easy as they were looked down upon as ignorant aliens. In the words of one immigrant "they make me laugh when they call us aliens. Don't they know that their ancestors were once aliens, too!" Perhaps subtle humor was an important ingredient for their survival.

Little Italy, as it came to be known, was settled just beyond the Irish and German enclaves of the near north. Besides working in the clay mines and making bricks, often they worked at V. Viviano's Macaroni Mfg. Co. which was located on the southeast corner of 7th and Carr. As a number of the immigrants used to be fruit peddlers in the old country, they fit right into the produce industry on nearby Commission Row (later called Produce Row). The women often worked in the garment district between 12th and 18th streets on Washington at places such as Curlee's Clothing Company that was owned by the Mercurio family. They lived in tenements from 6th Street West to 12th Street, from Franklin Avenue to Cass Avenue.

In 1899, a young Italian immigrant ar-

rived dressed in a black suit and a stiff, white collar. Father Cesare Spigardi, who was born in Mantova, Italy, on August 31st, 1889, was sent by Bishop Scalabrini to work with the struggling Italian immigrants. His parish was the entire city until Archbishop Glennon passed over some of his arduous load to Reverend Luciano Carotti. Father Spigardi instinctively recognized how hard it must have been for his compatriots, who had worked the land in Italy, to arrive in a strange country. Recognizing the needs, he once said, "There are thousands of immigrant Italians in St. Louis and very few of them can speak English. With no soil to till, they clean sewers, sell fish and produce on the streets, shine shoes, and work in the dark pits of the mines or the garment factories. They

*Postcard of Franklin Avenue, looking west from 7th Street in 1910. The Globe was a men's store.*

*The grandfather of local genealogist, Scott Biondo, is pictured in this little Italy scene of the local band that played at the majority of Italian weddings, dances, and festive occasions.*

*A postcard view of 6th Street looking south from Franklin Avenue toward Lucas, one of the streets that served as a shopping venue to the Little Italy community circa 1910.*

25

wanted to make a better life for themselves and their children." Father Spigardi understood these refugees looked to the parish, not only for sustenance for the soul, but for help in finding housing, jobs, citizenship, and lessons in English. For them, the parish was integral for survival of soul and body and, in return, the Catholic Church passed on the faith and suffered alongside them.

Immediately, the young Spigardi set to work and, with the strength born of his faith, he aided the poor and the sick. He used his own meager funds to provide them with groceries and clothing. Yet, Father Spigardi welcomed the rich into his arms as well. In order to cater to everyone's needs, a church was necessary.

Through his determination and hard work, Father Spigardi saw not one, but three churches built in Little Italy and on the Hill. He established Our Lady Help of Christians, a mission church that congregated in a former Methodist church at 1010 Cole Street. By 1902, St. Charles Borromeo on 29th and Locust streets rose up to welcome and protect the midtown immigrants. St. Ambrose Church on the Hill and St. Dominic's Orphanage was next added to his parish in 1903. Many in St. Louis took notice, including Adolphus Busch who showed his appreciation by giving Father Spigardi $10,000 to further aid his work.

The *New York Times* even recorded a sacrificial deed on December 16, 1900 when the newly established Our Lady Help of Christians caught fire. "Spigardi was rescued by firemen after he had fallen unconscious in the middle of the church, still clasping the ciborium containing the Eucharist in his hands," and he risked his life to run in and save the Holy Eucharist from destruction. Father Spigardi, when he

*Italian Baths at 88 Chestnut Street, in the Globe Shaving Parlor, opposite the post office. A notice in the* Missouri Republican *newspaper on June 10, 1845 states, "The proprietors return thanks to the citizens of St. Louis, and the public at large, for the very liberal patronage extended to them, and beg leave to inform them that they have connected to their Splendid Hair Cutting and Shaving Saloon, baths, in a style far superior to any in the city, and equal, if not superior to any in the United States. The tubs are of the finest Italian marble, the rooms large, airy, and elegantly furnished, and water clear as crystal. Gentlemen wishing a luxurious bath, an easy shave, or hair fashionably cut, are respectfully requested to call. Baths 25 cents."*

died from pneumonia on May 8th, 1931, was recognized as "the greatest leader of the Italians in the State of Missouri."

Following up on Father Spigardi's work in the late-1940s and 1950s was Father Carl Poelker at Our Lady Help of Christians.

As Father Spigardi had noted, the early tenements where Italians lived were dilapidated, in part, because landlords did not make improvements. But the living quarters, as described by housing reports maintain that the lodgings were kept clean "and in the windows there are often boxes or tin cans, holding carefully tended plants. When late afternoon comes the tables are carried outside and the alley is lined with family parties resting, drinking, and gossiping. The peddlers with their candy and cake push-carts make their way between."

In lieu of plumbing facilities, each family had their own key to an outdoor toilet. Up until the 1950s, baths had to be taken at the public bathhouse on 10th Street between Carr and Biddle. For two cents, one had the use of a bar of soap and a towel for drying.

Making their own amusements and entertainments, the boys were sent to Produce Row

*Rose's landmark restaurant at 10th and Franklin in Little Italy was a premier meeting place, especially for workers from Washington Avenue, the garment, fur, hat and shoe center of the Midwest. Later, a favorite after an evening aboard the* Admiral, *Rose's boasted long lines outside the door at 2:00 a.m. Great Southern Italian fresh dinners were served by chef Giuseppe Pugliese, at left, assisted by Michael La Monica and Steve Mondello (photo 1960). Rose's was originally Rosario's, established in 1927. In 1933, Jasper Bonaventure purchased it and changed the name to Rose's. Rose's closed in 1973.*

*Since the mid 1890s, the Rosciglione family had owned and operated a* dolceria *(bakery) and* sorbeteria *(ices) in Little Italy. Initially renting at 1011 ½ 7th street, the family eventually bought the entire city block. Pictured are Dominic Rosciglione, his brother and store owner, Francesco, and brother Tony, circa 1910.*

*The family of the pioneer pharmacist Louis Serra came to America on the ship* Madonna *in 1913. It took seven difficult and lonely years for his father to save enough money to send for them. Love conquered all when his wife, Rose, and their two children, Louis and Mary, arrived from Fuggia, Italy.*

27

to collect wood for the fire and since vegetables were usually packed in wooden crates, there was plenty of firewood to last the night. Families then enjoyed delicious outdoor barbeques, placing the wood inside big porcelain washtubs, a grate on top, and grilling their meats, community style. In addition, tomatoes were pulled from shared garden plots and everyone helped to season and boil them, then communally share the delicious, savory sauce produced.

*Joe Cusumano, of the Kemoll's Restaurant Cusumanos, delivered produce from his wagon throughout Little Italy in 1915.*

One of the main events of the early colony was the celebration of the Congregation of Santa Fara, the patroness of the town of Cinisi. The festival was held in the month of April when solemn vespers were sung followed by a colorful parade and musical accompaniment by Little Italy's Drum Corps or band. In later

decades, many remember the processions on Good Friday and on St. Joseph's Day at Our Lady Help of Christians or the honoring of a saint from a particular town in Italy. As the statue was carried through the streets, people pinned money on ribbons and this was used to help the poor, the sick, and the needy. Afterwards, at dusk, fireworks lit up the sky in Columbus Square Park

Regarding their children, immigrant parents were determined that the next generation receive a proper education. Many of their children attended school at either Patrick Henry Public at 12th and 10th, the only building in this area that was saved from the wrecker's ball, or St. Patrick's Parochial.

While the children were in school the mothers went off to socialize around the olive barrels at the Italo-American General Store, which sold items like 30 different-shaped pastas, beans, and West African palm oil to make the popular Sicilian palm soup. This emporium with its oils, wines, and delicatessen was opened in 1915 by James Lito and Frank Corro, with Louie Ruggeri also a partner, in the 500 block of Franklin. In later years, this market moved to 5851 Elizabeth

on the Hill. Also well frequented were: the Rome Drug Store, the Selvaggi and Coppolino steamship agency, Costa's Grocery, Bartolotta's Tavern, and Tocco's Fresh Fish Market. Friends gathered to dine at Jasper's Bar and Grill, once owned by the Sansone family, or at Rose's restaurant at 10th and Franklin. Rose's restaurant was run by Chef Joe Pugliese and owned by Jasper Bonaventure. Later in the 1960s, Joe opened up Guiseppe's at Meremac and Grand. Many also frequented Roma's restaurant and talked with Mamma Polizzi who always had time for a chat and would always tell everyone to visit her butcher shop next door. The local Sicilian family could buy mouth-watering cannoli at Rosciglione's or at Valenti's Bakery, and fresh meats at Monteleone's Meat Market. Nearby one could hear the cacophonous voices of street vendors calling, "Fish, *pesci freschi – che bella insalata* (Fresh fish and vegetables)!" For the freshest produce, the women of the house headed off to the Morreale Family Market on Carr between 9th and 10th.

At 8th and Carr was the Benincasa's Drug Store and at Pagano's Florist, 934-36 North 8 Street (telephone EVergreen 7350), Joe Pagano introduced to the neighborhood the concept of sending flowers to sick friends in the hospital. As one passed the Vincenzo "Pomo" Vivirito Tavern, it was easy to hear the raucous sound of men playing *zipponetta* and poker, with the animated owner smoking his Italian stogies, reminiscing about the "good old days" back in Italy.

The women of the house bought special-cut spiedini meat, steaks, soup bones, and great salsiccia at Tranchilla's on the corner of 9th and Carr. Indelicato's Grocery on 10th and

Pictured, at left, are Peter Rosciglione, Sr., Grandma Cosimina, and Grandpa Francesco in 1940 in front of their cake and pastry display counters. In the foreground are the cases holding the Italian ices and gelato for which the family was famous. The wrought iron café tables and display counters are used today by Peter and Pam Rosciglione in their fourth-generation bakery in St. Charles. Photo Below: Cass looking west from 10th in 1956.

Photo courtesy of the Missouri History Museum/Library and Research Center

Washington was the place to haggle over the price of artichokes.

Peter Rosciglione, whose grandfather settled in that area in the 1890s and remained in the neighborhood until the 1960s, owned the city block at 7th and Carr. Above the bakery and stores were 36 apartment units, each with a balcony and a big yard in back where children played. Peter remembers many family friends including the Bommaritos, Del Pietros, Olivastros, Randazzos, Pavias, Zerillos, and Zangaras, to name a few.

Sadly the City of St. Louis felt "the rabbit warren of tenement buildings" was an eyesore. In 1942, the city built housing projects from Carr to Cass and from 9th to 7th streets. Further redevelopment and the construction of the America's Center convention complex signaled the demise of Little Italy. Many of the business owners and evicted families sought greener pastures by migrating to the Hill, South and North County and even as far away as Du Quoin in Southern Illinois.

In a hurry to "Americanize" many parents encouraged their children to change their names from Giuseppe to Joe and Giovanni to John. The melting pot and progress had stolen a colorful history.

The stores, shops, churches, and families are gone. Officially, the last resident, Michael Barrone, left the last lonely row house at 9th and Cole in April 1976. The neighborhood no longer exists but wonderful memories, both painful and joyful, in the loss of this wonderful community of outstanding Italian immigrants still live in the hearts of their children.

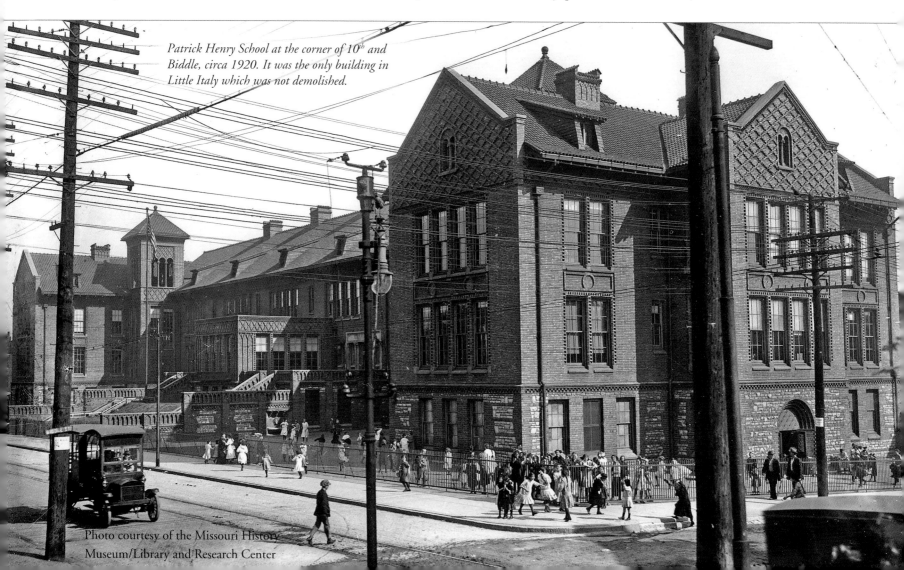

*Patrick Henry School at the corner of 10th and Biddle, circa 1920. It was the only building in Little Italy which was not demolished.*

Photo courtesy of the Missouri History Museum/Library and Research Center

*The 1927 funeral for Antonia Cusumano, wife of realtor and produce wholesaler Joe Cusumano, was one of the largest Little Italy had ever experienced. "Thousands of breathtaking flower arrangements flowed up and down the street in front of their home," according to Ellen Cusumano, co-owner of the legendary Kemoll's Restaurant.*

*Viviano Bros. Macaroni Manufacturing was located at 7th and Carr in the late 1920s and employed a number of Sicilians and Calabrians when they first immigrated to St. Louis' Little Italy.*

Photo courtesy of the Missouri History Museum/Library and Research Center

*Located at 8th and Poplar streets, Simmons Hardware employed a number of the residents of Little Italy.*

31

*The Columbus Day parade (Columbus statue in background) is one of the longest continuous-running parades in the country, originated by the Fratellanza Society in 1867. This photo, in the 1960s, shows the Knights of Columbus Honor Guard participating in the Columbus Day Parade, which, for almost 120 years, the parade route was between downtown and Tower Grove Park. In the park, a small ceremony was held at the base of the statue of Christopher Columbus. Beginning in the 1980s, the parade left Southwest Bank at Kingshighway and made its way to Berra Park.*

# FRATELLANZA

The Fratellanza, the Italian Union and Fraternal Society, organized with 64 members in St. Louis on November 12th, 1866 as a mutual aid society. Although the early Italian immigrants to St. Louis grew to love their new home in America, it became clear, particularly to fruit merchant Antonio Curotto, that the growing enclave needed support. By forming an association, the Italian community could help the newcomers acclimate, yet preserve their beloved Italian heritage. Hence, the birth of the Fratellanza Society, the Societa Unione e Fratellanza Italiana, incorporated on December 6, 1866.

The primary objective of the founders was "Unity of all St. Louis Italians" into a compact body devoted to common interests. In the early years when the Lombards (Northern Italians) and Sicilians faced a clash of cultures, especially while working in the mines, the Fratellanza mediated as well as imposed a $2.00 fine per fight. After a couple of generations, the old hostilities eventually dissipated.

In 1867, also to promote harmony and unity, the Society initiated the first Columbus Day Parade, one of the oldest, continuous-running parades in the country.

As well as unity, the scope of the Society included helping members "endure the vicissitudes of the pioneer life." Thus, in case of sickness or accident, the Fratellanza Benevolent Society paid $10.50 a week to members to help support their families. The organization also had its own doctors and dentists on call for distress situations.

In addition, the Society maintains permanent burial grounds for deceased members and their families.

The Fratellanza continues to thrive today, still maintaining the traditions of Italian heritage and culture in America. It is now open to members of all ethnic groups.

Counter-clockwise from above:

　　Pictured, left to right, in 1969, are Gino Mariani, Aldo Della Croce (singing), and Don Fanetti, the Bugle publisher from 1945-1970, who played Italian ballads at the annual Fratellanza picnic.

　　Photographed in 1940, Victor Zerega in front of the former Giovanni Frey Co. on Third Street at Walnut, where the Fratellanza was born.

　　The Italian Fraternal Building at Vandeventer and Delmar, established on December 6, 1925 was a popular meeting hall for many Italian-American organizations.

　　A recent Columbus Day Annual Parade and Festival.

　　Calvary Cemetery memorial services in 1969. Pictured are Lee Tessaro, at left, and his father, Louis Tessaro, at the graves of the Fratellanza.

# PRODUCE ROW

*A critical part of how the old market operated was the auction. The auction building, current location of the casino, one block north, is where all the action was. Buyers would come into the produce building (photo) to inspect and taste the product displayed in sample lots, where they picked up the lot numbers.*

*The east side of 4th and Franklin looking south, home to the original Produce Row. The Wabash Railroad in the pre-1960 years built and maintained extensive storage facilities beside their tracks. "As colorful as Old Man River," says Charles Gallagher, Sr., owner of United Fruit and Produce Co., referring to the activity of Produce Row. Knowing the history of the market, he adds, "Before Soulard Market there was the French Market where they sold live chickens, skinned rabbit, coon, and possum. A law was passed, still on the books today, that the fur had to be left on the right paw to determine what kind of skinned animal was actually being purchased."*

Lombardo, Sanfilippo, Giordano, Catanzaro, Cusumano, Pagano, Pupillo, Ventimiglia, Mantia, Curotto. Just a few Italian-American names that have, over the years, dominated the St. Louis fruit markets also known as Produce or Commission Row. In 1918, Gould's Directory listed 35 Italian fresh fruit merchants, all of whom lived in Little Italy, which bordered the great open-air markets. Many of the Sicilians working in the stalls had previous experience in the old country. Produce Row was inaugurated by families of produce purveyors. For example, in 1946, Frank Cusumano opened Franklin

34

Produce at Fourth and Franklin Avenue. With brother, Sam, and son, Francis Paul, the family built the business in the '50s and '60s, catering to not only Wetterau and A&P, but also to numerous corner groceries and peddlers who hawked produce in neighborhoods. "Frank Cusumano was the patriarch of the Row," according to owner, Jack Cusumano. "He was a hardworking man of integrity, well respected, good hearted, and never failing to reach out to help others become established and successful." Although times have changed and many wholesalers have taken on partners outside the

family, at Franklin Produce, the business is still conducted solely by the Cusumano family members - Jack, Francis, and cousins to several others in the local food trade, including to the Cusumano clan that runs the famous Kemoll's Restaurant.

Produce Row opened at its current location on February 3, 1953, though it existed elsewhere, under different names, long before that. In the time of Laclede and Chouteau, a loosely formed market was, by convenience, located along the levee, where merchants were able to meet the boats carrying commodities up

3rd and Cole Street, looking south of Produce Row. This whole area was demolished to make room for the new Veteran's (renamed Martin Luther King, Jr.) Bridge. From 8 p.m. till 4 a.m. the place was a chaotic beehive of activity with trucks, many independents unloading, buying, auctioning, and loading the trucks, readying before morning rush hour to drop off to all the grocers, hospitals, nursing homes, and even produce to feed the St. Louis Zoo animals. Al's Steak House was birthed at First and Biddle in Little Italy to cater to the market traffic.

Pictured is the approach to the Eads Bridge in 1893, where produce building and fruit peddler wagons abounded. This scene is adjacent to Little Italy, which bordered the great open-air markets. Italian fresh fruit merchants from the 1860s on worked here in vast numbers as many of the Sicilians working the stalls had previous experience in the old country.

One of the oldest Italian purveyors in the market in the new Produce Row established in 1953 is Gus (Augusto) Mantia. In his late 80s, Italians like him and Anthony Ventimiglia who retired from the market, still come in every day to be part of the excitement. Daily, the volume of produce that comes into Produce Row from 49 states and 74 countries is valued at 2 million dollars.

and down the Mississippi. Then, around 1875, the merchants moved their stores to a 36-acre tract along Third and Fourth streets between Biddle on the north and Washington. The place became known as Commission Row, a conglomerate of homes and business storefronts converted to stalls where meat and poultry were sold alongside fruits and vegetables.

By the late '40s, construction of what is now the Martin Luther King Bridge began displacing some business. The merchants banded together, forming the St. Louis Fruit and Produce Association. They pooled their resources and, in 1950, with the purchase of land from the Wabash Railroad, began the construction of a wholesale terminal market. The new facility, with high ceilings for upward storage, had railroad tracks coming right up to the back docks. The produce came by boxcar up until the 1960s. In the late '50s and early '60s, the trucks started rolling in. Today the 21.5 acre complex, located on North Market one block east of North Broadway, sees some 18,000 tractor-trailers per year. Produce Row is going full-tilt when most are asleep. It is a trading hub that takes in buyers from about 150 miles in all directions, making Produce Row a veritable fruit basket to the Midwest.

Some purveyors also have charity as well as commerce in mind. The Cusumano family have donated generously to The Little Sisters of the Poor, the Sisters of Sacred Heart Villa, St. Patrick's and The Shrine of St. Joseph Catholic Churches. "This has been going on for years," says Fran and Jack Cusumano. "We stuff their vans with fruits and vegetables," they remark proudly, "and it's the best stuff, not your throwaway produce."

*Photo right: Joe Sanfilippo (at right) with Frank Palozolla (standing at left). The friends worked alongside each other in Soulard Market from the 1940s to the 1970s. Joseph Leopold Sanfilippo, long associated with Soulard Farmers' Market (market photo at left from the 1950s) as well as with Anthony's Produce, is acknowledged for his apprenticeship of current local produce distributors and buyers. His father "Mr. Pete" and Uncle Joseph, who came from Trappeto, Sicily in 1911, used to vend produce on pushcarts through the city. After the brothers brought over their wives, the Ciaramitaro sisters, the latter two pioneered as working women in the oldest market west of the Mississippi.*

*Joe Cusumano, whose store was laden with fresh produce and flowers, is photographed outside of his establishment at 915 North Broadway Street. In the photo, Joe Cusumano is identified, at left, next to his nephew, Frank, who would, a few years later, marry Mary Grace Kemoll, daughter of the founders of Kemoll's Restaurant.*

# ITALIANS AT 1904 WORLD'S FAIR

The official opening of the Italian National Pavilion took place on June 6, 1904. From 4-6 p.m. that day, visitors walked up the wide stairs through the Ionic columns into a pavilion designed to resemble an ancient marble villa of a Roman emperor.

Along with priceless paintings, the Italian Government sent to the exhibition rare collections of marble statues, carved furniture, and bronzes. Visitors walked through the pavilion's reception room to view replica statues from the ruins of Herculaneum and Pompeii along with modern works of art. This extraordinary se-

ries of displays was valued at $3,000,000 in 1904. The Italian Government took home some of the most coveted prizes given to individual countries. Further recognition occurred on October 12, 1904, the 412th anniversary of the discovery of America by Christopher Columbus, which was Italian Day at the fair.

On the walls inside the pavilion, huge banners hung which chronicled the history of the Roman Empire until the discovery of America. St. Louis Italians took great pride in the rare art and culture displayed, which for centuries had been a source of inspiration for art and sculpture throughout Europe. During the Fair, concerts featuring Italian music entertained fair visitors and special guests in the pavilion. Exceptional gardens surrounded the Italian buildings. Also popular was the Italian restaurant in the West Pavilion which could seat over 2,000 diners at a time.

*During the 1904 World's Fair, those visiting the Italian Pavilion could make purchases from the Italian homeland in the pictured Italy Department of Manufacturing building. Photos courtesy of the Missouri History Museum/Library and Research Center.*

Early (Italian) immigrants lived in the northern edge of the Hill area around Pattison, Northrup, and Shaw. During the 1890s, Lombards, or Northern Italians, arrived in a constant stream. Many worked in the clay plants and, because the workers had to live close to the mine, the Fairmont section built up rapidly. By 1900, Sicilians discovered the Hill. Although the Lombards outnumbered Sicilians three to one, two languages were used in the mines and factories. This inaugurated a generation of bitter ethnic quarreling.

The area was remote from the city center and public utilities were virtually non-existent. Many lived in the old shotgun frame shanties which had only three rooms each. Some lived in boxcars until the mine companies built the shanties. After the turn of the century, one-story, four-room brick houses appeared. These were for single men who married later on or for married men who had sent for their families. These residences were overflowing most of the time as men would pack in wherever they could

> *"As a result of experience I rate the Italian highly and consider him a most desirable immigrant."*
>
> Andrew Carnegie

and they lived and worked in shifts. In 1890, the Hill's residential district consisted of ten austere shacks. 175 men were found living in

34 rooms. Most of the early homes served as boarding houses. The boarding house system outlived its usefulness by the 1920s. Some homes had ten boarders at one time. The men slept in cramped quarters, often on cots, five and six to a room. Money earned served as a means of support for the host family.

During that (1920s) period, 999 homes were built on the Hill. The next decade added another 321 units. The national census of 1930 recorded virtually no boarders on the Hill.

From 1848 through the end of the 19th Century, clay mining and brick-making was the central thrust of the economy which kept this neighborhood going, and which accounted for the growth of population. Both mining and brick-making continued into the 20th century, but mining was definitely waning and most mines were closed by the mid-1930s. Until 1960, bricks continued to be made by Laclede-Christy on Chippewa; Evans and Howard on Manchester; Laclede #1, at Wilson Avenue near Sulphur; and

Blackmer-Post on Columbia and Hereford. But in the whole of the 20th Century, both mining and brick-making were secondary factors in the local economy and were not much of an impetus for new people to settle in the area.

In 1908, the yearly output of clay products for the city was valued at $6.4 million. An expert geologist once remarked that Cheltenham clay could easily be used in the manufacture of the finest pottery in the world. But the local industries preferred sewer pipe and fire brick which, rather than attracting master potters, attracted thousands of unskilled laborers. In the peak years of mining (1860-1930s), everything was done by hand. The worker would go straight down a shaft in a cage. They worked in what they called a stall. They had to furnish their own drill, pick, shovel, and dynamite. After digging with a pick, getting 35/40 cents a ton, the clay was loaded in a boxcar then pulled by mules to the cage. An intricate tunnel network was developed. After a day's work, they would put the dynamite in holes and break up the clay when they left for the next day's work. The mules were a small white breed of the Missouri mule. They were kept in the tunnel, went blind and died there.

The clay was white and porous and was removed like chunks of coal. It seemed the clay was deeper than coal although it was found between layers of limestone. Once the "cager" transferred the clay to the outside, it was loaded onto cars and taken to the factory yards for up to three years of curing. Once cured, it would be ground and pulverized, rubbed through a screen, then made into bricks.

The Cheltenham Industrial Complex dominated the local economy until the 1930s. "Every morning," wrote columnist Harry Brundidge in 1936, "an army of workers stepped down the steep paths to work in the mines and factories." The Hill, in the early 1900s, became one of the most stable economies in the city since there was very little transiency. In a 1935 study, Donald Cowgill called the Hill "Fairmont Heights."

In 1900, 90% of the Hill's male workforce (325 men) was employed at the Cheltenham brickworks. By the Depression, only 30% labored there. In 1900, a brick worker's pay was $1.35 to $1.50 per day. The pay had hardly changed since the 1890s.

Gradually, the Italians found other work. The simultaneous exhaustion of the clay mines and the Great Depression devastated the Cheltenham brick, tile, and mining industries. In 1930, 17% of the factory workers in the area were unemployed or laid off without pay. The employment situation would worsen, and by the time the A.F.L. was strong enough to unionize the industry, the Cheltenham kilns were cold. Later, the mines were used for dumping grounds and the factories have long since changed owners. But the last of Cheltenham's occupants, the descendants of Lombards and Sicilians, felt comfortable remaining in the old neighborhood.

During the period after 1910, heavy and light industries gravitated to the Cheltenham locale. Two of the most important sources of employment were the Carondelet Foundry and the Banner Iron Works, which by 1930

employed 11% of the colony's males (205 jobs). In 1910, the Quick Meal Stove Company, which introduced the gas-burning Magic Chef Oven in 1929, erected an immense factory at 2100 Kingshighway and employed more than 100 Hill workers during the 1920s and 1930s. Joining the industrial network was the McQuay-Norris Company, which built a spacious plant at Southwest Avenue and Cooper in 1919. The factory manufactured piston rings and engine parts and employed 75 residents in 1930.

*–Excerpted from the writings of Louis H. Schmidt*

*Delivering coal to mines in the Cheltenham Industrial Complex, circa early 1900s.*

*Photo Opposite Page: Italians and African Americans working together in the clay mines in Fairmont Heights [The Hill area]. Photo courtesy of the Missouri History Museum/Library and Research Center.*

# THE HILL

"A feeling for community continues to intertwine the lives of Hill inhabitants, just as it had many years earlier."

*Gary Ross Mormino*

The geographic location of the Hill in the City of St. Louis is bounded by Kingshighway, Northrup, January, and Southwest Avenue. In 1890, both the Frisco and the Missouri-Pacific Railroads began running through the northern portion of the Hill, known as the Fairmont District. Railroads became a catalyst for business growth and industry expansion. As a result, the increased need for labor drew many Italian immigrants to the Hill.

From 1880 to 1895, records indicate the names of the first Italians who settled on the Hill were: Luigi Oldani; Domenico Taveggia; Luigi Caloia; Paolo Re; Luigi Enrico, and Carlo Berra; Luigi Giacomo; Carlo Gualdoni; Abramo, Carlo, and Angelo Calcaterra; Cesare Oldani; Dionigi Puricelli; Domenica Miriani; Allesandro Chiodini; Calogero Mugavero; Pietro Mazzola; and Theodore Brusatore.

Around 1900, the Hill recorded 600 Italians, mostly male, mostly bachelors. They desired to build a new life for themselves and their families to follow. So, they journeyed here; filled with dreams of a better life.

At the turn of the 20th Century, the community boasted a general store, a bakery, a saloon, a Garibaldi society, and an anti-Garibaldi society. The Lombard dialect was heard everywhere and especially during mass in a rented

40

portion of a local German-Catholic Church. This was before the founding of St. Ambrose Church which became the cornerstone of the Hill community.

Weekly streams of new arrivals between 1900 and 1914 augmented the population. Despite the temporary halt in immigration during World War I and the repatriation of some immigrants to their homeland by 1920, the Hill and Little Italy was home to 18,000 foreign-born Italians and second-generation residents.

The Italian work ethic was the impetus which made the Hill a viable part of the City of St. Louis. Daily, these tired and weary men trudged up the steep, muddy hill on their way home from the mines. Since they believed the Hill was the highest point in the City of St. Louis, they referred to it as *La Montagna* (The Mountain). After 10 or 12 hours of hard labor, their trek home certainly must have been similar to climbing an actual mountain!

In the early 1900s, the Hill was geographically isolated from mainstream St. Louis life, lying close to the city's western border. City services such as paved streets, sewers, and streetlights were non-existent.

The Hill slowly became a self-sufficient neighborhood. With financial security, the immigrant workers fulfilled their primary goal and built their own private residences. The city did its part by paving streets, bringing in water and sewer lines, and providing schools, mail carriers, and police officers. Between the years of 1900 and 1920, numerous small businesses began to flourish. It was during this period that the Hill became totally self-sufficient. Mercantile establishments were started out of necessity to meet people's basic needs—shoe repair shops, bakeries, a grocery store on every corner, taverns, doctors, barbershops, drugstores, a funeral parlor, dry goods, and furniture stores. And even entertainment with movie theaters and their own brass band. Many original set-

tlers never left the neighborhood because everything they needed was here including a "continuity of culture, the commonality of their own language, and the cohesiveness of group/kin/family solidarity." As one resident asserts, "My Mom must have been fifty years old before she crossed Kingshighway." However, when anyone wanted to venture downtown, in the 1940s, bus service on the Russell Line was available. Post-World War II, the Hill enjoyed every modern convenience such as "radios, automobiles, furniture, bicycles, skates, theater, fine apparel, and proximity to Forest Park Highlands for summer diversion."

The City of St. Louis also responded to the wishes of Hill residents by changing the name of Cooper Street to Marconi in memory of Guglielmo Marconi, inventor of the telegraph, who had died in 1937.

During the challenge of the Depression years, the Hill community fared better than most neighborhoods. As Father Anthony Pa-

*Dedication of the new St. Ambrose School in 1950. Included in the picture are Bishop Charles Koester, Monsignor Palumbo, Calogero Mancuso, John Calavenna, Charley Garavaglia, Henry Ruggeri, David Fontana, Dr. Charles Montani, Charles Clavenna, Paul Calcaterra, Father Raymond Diermann, Archbishop Ritter, Louis "Midge" Berra, Cosmo Giudici, and others.*

41

lumbo explained, "People were willing to help one another because they knew one another. Moreover, the main dish was spaghetti, so there was no real problem with food."

This sense of tight-knit community held true when, in the late 1970s, Washington University sociologists questioned Hill residents' depth of feeling regarding their neighborhood. Over 80 percent of the respondents expressed a high degree of satisfaction in the neighborhood and 90 percent maintained a strong feeling of community. "Incredibly, in a nation dedicated to novelty and newness, the Hill has retained the essential vestiges of its ancestors: the neighborhood remains working class and Italian." Modernity in combination with community continues to make the Hill a unique model neighborhood.

*Louis P. Serra became a successful pharmacist at Marconi and Daggett. He married Anna DiLiberta.*

*The Belmonde Tavern on Watson was owned by Joseph Italian. His grandson, Joe, remembers many stories; one time his father, Vincent, fell out of the cherry tree near the tavern, causing his Dad, Joseph, great concern.*

*The photo above looks east over the construction site of the Southwest Avenue viaduct. The project was begun in 1913 and completed in 1920. The building on the left eventually became Favazza's restaurant on the corner of Marconi and Southwest.*

*Acolytes/Altar Boys in the 1930s: Back Row, left to right: Nat Lucido, Vito Polizzi, Dominic Biondo, Joseph Polizzi, Vince de Blaze, Unknown, Gus Torre Grosso, and Tom Valenza. Front row, left to right: Unknown, Anthony Aiello, Charlie Lombardo, Father Filipiak, Sal Giuffrida, Unknown, Unknown.*

# Familiar Places

Familiar places—where St. Louisans enjoy good times with friends and neighbors at sandwich shops, taverns, bakeries, and delis—places held dear to many hearts. Not to mention the great ham, salsiccia, meatball, and roast beef sandwiches, and cannoli for relatively low prices along with an atmosphere rich with nostalgia and memorabilia. Family-run businesses, the owners work tirelessly to serve the best with good humor. Quaint and original, these places are landmarks. Plus, the food and treats are worth the trip.

# Joe Fassi's

*Photo Above: Owner Tom Call, great-grandson of Papa Paulo Fassi, holds up his #1 best-selling meatball sandwich along with his Pranzo salad. In the background is a painting of 2323 Sublette which was first purchased by Papa Paul in 1926. Bottom photo is Fassi Tavern as it appeared in the 1940s.*

Papa Paulo Fassi emigrated from Milan in Lombardy. When he arrived in St Louis in 1900, his Lombardy father arranged a marriage and sent over a bride, Rosa Carettoni. When the ambitious Papa Paul earned enough money, he fulfilled his dream and purchased property at 2323 Sublette, the roots of what is today the Joe Fassi Sausage and Sandwich Factory. Papa Paul, current owner Tom Coll's great grandfather, established a grocery business in 1926. Joe was Papa Paul's eldest, who along with his brothers Louis, Vince, Emil and Paul and their wives Mary, Jennie, Frances, Mary, and Marie supplied the original work crew. This sizable staff divided their time between an ice cream parlor and pool hall, which occupied half the Sublette site, along with the grocery store. After Prohibition the ice cream parlor transitioned into a tavern. The business prospered and "Uncle Vince" continued until 1992.

At that point, nephew Tom Coll stepped forward and with a little help from his Aunt Jennie Fassi, Lou's wife, Joe Fassi Sausage and Sandwich Factory was born. "I remember" says Tom, "as kids we met once a week in the basement and Uncle Vince would grind and mix the sausage and we kids formed a production line to stuff the sausages." Currently with Tom's mother, Rose, the production line every three weeks dishes up a 400-pound batch of meatballs, which, according to Tom, continues to be their #1 bestselling sandwich. Also popular is the Yogi Berra Hot Dog Special, created in honor of a *Show Me St. Louis* Channel 9 feature which commemorated a slice of life Hill scene: Yogi Berra and Joe Garagiola as young boys making a mad dash for the Fassi Tavern when the 4:30 whistle blew to pick up a "tureen" of beer for their working dads.

## JOE FASSI'S FAMOUS PRANZO SALAD

*1 large head Romaine lettuce*  
*1 large head of green leaf lettuce*  
*10 pepperoncinis*  
*2 large tomatoes, cut in quarters*  
*2 cups Parmesan cheese*  
*1 cup Fassi's olive salad*  

*1 cup sliced black olives*  
*½ cup diced pimentos*  
*5 artichoke hearts, cut in quarters*  
*¼ lb. Italian salami, cut in slices*  
*½ lb. baked ham, cut in pieces*  
*6 oz. Fassi's Italian dressing*  

Cut and wash lettuce. Add all of the above ingredients, with dressing added last. Toss in a large bowl and serve. Serves 8-10.

# *Rosciglione's*

Vincenzo Rosciglione came to Little Italy in St Louis in 1895 from Palermo, Sicily and opened a coffee and pastry shop. In 1904, he brought over his son, Francesco, who had been studying to be a pastry chef in Sicily. Francesco was thrilled to be able to attend the St. Louis World's Fair and being particularly gifted artistically, he introduced the old-country custom of making sugar dolls. His son Pietro (Peter) took over and realized his dream by purchasing the whole city block the bakery rested upon. In 1968, Rosciglione Bakery followed its customer base to Dellwood in North County. Peter, Jr. took over the reins of the family business in 1980 assisted by his wife, Pam, and daughter, Gina. Suddenly the opportunity to re-ignite the family dream arose in 1987, when they purchased a 1-acre site in St. Charles. There they built a facility to continue baking the mouth-watering pastries, cookies, and signature cannolis, prepared from homemade shells and fillings. As if to mark an unbroken link to the past, Pam Rosciglione lovingly restored the original counters and cookie cases, currently on display at their St. Charles location.

Not only that, the link to the old country revived when the family discovered the relatives Papa Vincenzo left behind 100 years ago in Sicily had led parallel lives–also becoming bakers with an almost identical product line and even naming their sons, Vincenzo and Pietro down to the third generation! [Learn more about the Rosciglione family history in the Little Italy section of this book on page 22.]

## HONEY CLUSTERS (*STRUFOLI*)

| | | |
|---|---|---|
| *2 cups sifted flour* | *3 eggs* | *1 cup honey* |
| *¼ tsp. salt* | *¼ tsp. vanilla* | *1 tbsp. sugar* |

Combine dry ingredients. Add one egg at a time and vanilla until dough is soft. Turn dough onto a lightly floured surface and knead. Divide dough into halves. Lightly roll the first half ¼ in. thick to form a rectangle. Cut dough with a pastry cutter into strips ¼ in. wide. Use palm of hand to roll strips to pencil thickness. Cut into pieces about ¼ to ½ in. long. Deep fry 365° 3 to 5 min. Drain on absorbent paper. Cook in skillet over low heat for about 5 min: 1 cup honey, 1 tbsp. of sugar. Add deep-fried pieces and coat. Refrigerate to chill slightly. Remove to a large serving platter and arrange in a cone-shape mound. Sprinkle with 1 tbsp. of tiny, multicolored nonpareils. Serves 8 to 10.

*Photo Above: Peter and Pam Rosciglione show their strufoli. Below: Peter Rosciglione's grandfather, Francesco, was truly an artist when it came to making sugar dolls for the Rosciglione Bakery, a craft he brought from his native Sicily.*

*Above: Vitale's Italian Seed cookies are local favorites, according to owner, Grace Vitale.*
*Below: In 1947, the first generation, comprised of Peter and Frances Bommarito, opened Bommarito's Bakery.*

# Vitale's Bakery

Grace Vitale quotes Hawthorne: "Unbounded courage and self-determination is the stuff that heroes are made of." My father, Peter Bommarito, son of Italian immigrants possessed both qualities. He was determined to start his own business and he had the courage to do so.

In 1947, my parents, Peter and Frances, opened Bommarito's Bakery, on 18th and Madison. Their primary business was baking bread for all the restaurants in the city of St. Louis along with several import stores and markets in the growing downtown area.

As our business started to grow, my mother started selling the freshly baked bread in the front of the bakery during the day. When I was dating my future husband Pete Vitale, he was interested in baking, so my father, who took great pride in his baking, taught him the trade.

In 1966, my dad decided it was time to retire. Pete and I, along with my siblings, Sam and Josie, continued the tradition until 1975.

From there, Vitale's Bakery was born on the Hill, at 2130 Marconi. Vitale's continued baking bread for the restaurants throughout the city. The high demand helped the business to expand to a retail store to sell to customers.

Our bakery has become more than simply bread. We now make our traditional sesame seed, anise and biscotti to name a few cookies along with our cannolis.

Our cookie making during the holidays was a family affair. Kneading, rolling and decorating with seeds and sprinkles. I always looked at the cookie making not as making delicious sweets but works of art baked with love.

Our regular customers still come in to visit. They are really more than customers: they are part of our "family."

My parents would be proud that we have kept their baking tradition alive and that we honor the courage and determination they demonstrated over half a century ago.

## VITALE'S ITALIAN SEED COOKIES

1 cup sugar
1 cup shortening
3 eggs
1 tsp. vanilla
1 tsp. baking
    powder
2 cups flour
1 cup sesame
    seeds

Cream together sugar, shortening, eggs and vanilla. Add baking powder and flour. Mix until well combined. Roll evenly in two or three portions on waxed paper into log 1 to 1-1/2 inches in diameter. Roll up in waxed paper. Close ends. Refrigerate several hours or overnight.

Carefully unroll waxed paper, as dough still may be rather soft. Sprinkle sesame seeds over top of roll and on waxed paper along one side of roll. Gently roll over dough so all sesame seeds are on bottom. Add more sesame seeds to top.

Preheat oven to 375 degrees. Cut dough in 1½-inch lengths. Lay bundles on shiny baking sheets left ungreased or lined with parchment paper. Bake in preheated oven 8 to 10 minutes until lightly browned at edge. Makes about 30 cookies.

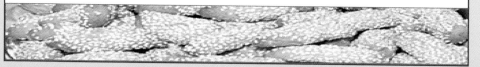

# Viviano's Festa Italiano

In 1950, John Viviano opened John Viviano & Sons on the Hill. His grandson, Michael, remembers, "My grandfather once told me, 'You have the business in your heart. You will live up to and help carry on the Viviano name in St. Louis.'" He took this prophecy to heart.

It all started at the turn of the last century when the patriarch, John, in his teens, immigrated to St. Louis. Later, he met and married Angela LoChirco. Grandson, Michael, was born on Marconi Avenue and spent long hours learning the trade from his father and grandfather, while working at Viviano's on the Hill. "After I married Beth, we moved to Fenton and saw that community growing and people looking for a great Italian market closer to home. In 2003, with sister-in-law, Becky Parker, Michael and Beth opened Viviano's Festa Italiano in Fenton Plaza on November 1, All-Saints Day, and were truly thankful for their blessings.

"It was our version of the Italian grocery, deli, and cafeteria. In 2007, we opened a second location in Chesterfield and were welcomed with open arms!" Michael, whose enthusiasm is contagious, invites one and all to enjoy a piece of Italy in their neighborhood, to savor the sights and sounds of a traditional Italian market "Where every day is an Italian Festival."

---

## PENNE ROMA

6 tbsp. extra virgin olive oil

1½ cups chopped onion

2 tsp. minced garlic

3 28-oz. cans Italian plum tomatoes, drained

2 tsp dried basil

1 1/2 tsp dried crushed red pepper

2 cups canned low-salt chicken broth

1/2 cup chopped pitted brine-cured olives
   (such as Kalamata)

1 lb. penne

2 ½ cups packed grated Havarti cheese

1/2 cup grated Parmesan cheese

1/4 cup finely chopped fresh basil

Heat three tablespoons oil in heavy pot over medium-high heat. Add onion and garlic; sauté until onion is translucent, about five minutes. Mix in tomatoes, dried basil, olives, and crushed red pepper. Bring to boil, breaking up tomatoes with back of spoon. Add broth. Reduce heat to medium; simmer for about two hours until sauce thickens. Season with salt and pepper to taste.

Preheat oven to 375 degrees. Cook pasta in large pot of boiling salted water until tender but still firm to bite. Drain well.

Return pasta to same pot. Toss with remaining three tablespoons oil. Pour sauce over and toss to blend. Mix in Havarti cheese. Transfer pasta to 13x9x2-inch glass baking dish. Sprinkle with Parmesan.

Bake until pasta is heated through, about 30 minutes. Sprinkle with basil.

SERVES 6

*Photo Top: Owners Mike Viviano with sister-in-law, Becky Parker. Featured is a family favorite, Penne Roma, a Sicilian dish that Mike's wife, Beth, has adapted for the cafe. Photo Above: Mike's grandparents, Angela and John Viviano, who would have been proud to know that a fourth generation of helping hands, comprised of Beth and Mike's son, Zachary Viviano, and Becky's daughters, Rachel and Christa Parker, have recently come on board.*

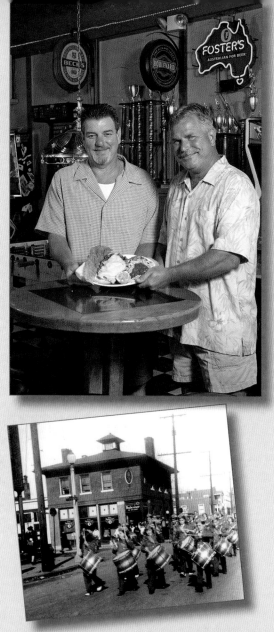

# Milo's Bocce Garden

On the corner of Wilson and Marconi a tavern was built and operated by Anheuser-Busch as early as 1902. With the onset of Prohibition, it was considered a bad investment to continue operation. So the business was sold and purchased by the Merlo family and was named Merlo's. In Italy, Merlo and his family were farmers and worked pitching hay. When he came to America he was known as Forchett, relating to his use of the pitchfork, *forchetta*. Mr. Merlo was a very religious man. He was famous for not serving drinks whenever a service was conducted in St. Ambrose Church. His motto was "You don't drink when you should be praying!"

In the 1950s, after the death of Mr. Merlo, his sons, Joe and Henry, ran the business. Following their ownership, the building was believed to be a tavern owned by Abel Pezzani, more often referred to as "Toots" Pezzani. Toots ran the business until it was taken over by Joe "Bull" Panneri. So in the '60s the bar was then named "Wil-Mar Lounge" because it was the corner of Wilson and Marconi. During the period that the bar was owned by Joe Panneri he took on partners including Gene "P. I." Pisoni and Charles "Butch" Grassi. Around 1975 Joe Panneri and Butch Grassi sold the business to Tom Savio and Joe Calcaterra and again the name changed to Milo's Tavern. Later in '78 Tom and Joe dissolved their partnership, leaving Tom Savio and his family to run the enterprise.

In 1989, Savio sold half the business to Joseph Vollmer. At this time they added Bocce courts and a full kitchen. Fortunately, every time the business was sold the new proprietors were families from the Hill neighborhood.

Basically the business has not changed from the little corner tavern patronized by tired, Italian immigrant men stopping for a drink with friends after long hours working in the mines and brickyards. Milo's remains an oasis for anyone wishing to share a drink and lively conversation - just like the early immigrants who pioneered the neighborhood.

*Top Photo: Partners since 1989, Tom Savio and Joseph Vollmer are proud to display their popular salsiccia sandwich at Milo's Tavern, which is also known as the sports center of the Hill. Once a center for men's class-A slow-pitch, Milo's now boasts a total of 58 bocce teams. Bottom Photo: The tavern as it appeared in 1958.*

## ITALIAN SALSICCIA SANDWICH

½ lb. Imo's salsiccia with fennel
¼ green pepper, sliced in strips
¼ white onion, sliced in strips

2 slices Provel cheese
Italian bread dipped in olive oil
1 tbsp. olive oil

Sauté green peppers and onion in olive oil. Set aside. Grill salsiccia to taste, cover with Provel cheese. Place on Italian bread and cover with sautéed vegetables. Serves one.

# Marconi Bakery

According to Sam Licata: Life in my little town, Lecare Friddi, Sicily was hard. When I was only eight, I worked carrying water to our town's bakery and was paid in bread. When I was fourteen, I had to quit school to help support our family.

I got a job working outside a sulphur mine. Sometimes sulphuric acid would rise to the top level where we worked. It was poisonous!

When I was twenty, my sister Angeline and I went to live with my aunt and uncle in America. They helped me get a job at La Rosa's bakery as well as at the spaghetti factory. When La Rosa sold his bakery to Ruma and Peluso, I was learning how to be a baker.

Life in America was good to me. When I was twenty-two I married my beautiful wife Barbara Puricelli. We have four children, Rose, Sam, Diane, and Maria and grandchildren Melissa and Sam ,Jr.

In 1969, we bought the bakery from Ruma and Peluso. I've always taught my children "Success only comes when you work hard!" They learned that life doesn't always give you what you want. I tell them "Come viene, si conta. (Take things as they come)." So each one has worked in the bakery at one time or another. They either helped with deliveries or learned how to make bread.

I learned that having your own business is hard. All through the heartaches and headaches that come with long hours, I still enjoy baking and feeling proud that I put out the best bread I'm capable of making.

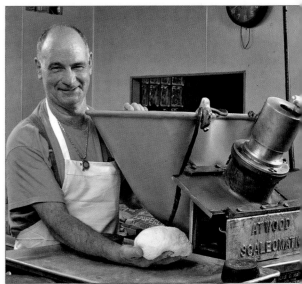

*Photo Above: Sam Licata, a craftsman at work at his bakery. Photo Below: Sam visiting with his sisters, Angie Mondello, at left, and Pietra Laforte.*

## MARCONI BREAD*

1 1/4 cups warm water
1 tbsp. butter, softened
1 tbsp. white sugar

1 tsp. salt
3 cups bread flour
1 (.25 ounce) package active dry yeast

In a bowl add warm water. Sprinkle yeast on top and set aside. Add softened butter to yeast. Blend together. Add dry ingredients. Place onto a floured surface. Knead for 8 - 10 minutes. (Or mix dough in the mixer for about 10 minutes.) Place dough into a lightly greased bowl. Cover with a cloth and proof for about one hour (let sit until doubled). Punch down gently. Cut dough in half. Place into 2 loaf pans. Cover and let rise again. Bake at 400 F. for 30-35 minutes. Cool on a wire rack.

*The original recipe was created by Mr. La Rosa when he opened the bakery in 1959. Sam Licata bought the bakery in 1969 and changed the recipe to the way it is now.

# Hill Top Inn

According to Rosalie LaGates: When my maternal grandfather came to America the immigration officer asked his name. He said "Philipe Cucchi," but the officer wrote "Philip Cook." My father, Joseph Garavaglia, married Julia Cook in 1939. Six months after their wedding they started a little business on Morganford in South St. Louis called The Hill Top Inn.

I was born in 1942 and that year my father went off to fight in World War II. This meant my Mom had to run the business alone. So my grandmother Rosa and my zia Theresa came to stay and help my mother. Grandma spoke little English so I became fluent in English and Italian.

When my father was in the army he was a mess sergeant. Returning to St. Louis he started back to work at our restaurant. In the early 1950s the farms surrounding Hill Top began fading away. The building boom was great for business construction companies. Their laborers sat alongside the white collar clientele enjoying Papa's meatballs, pasta, and especially ham cut from the bone.

I was 17 when my father died and once again my mother ran the business. When I was 24 I bought the business.

Hill Top has gone through major remodeling, all of which was done with the help of aunts, uncles, cousins, sons, and daughters-in-law. My husband, Al, retired from the St. Louis Police Department 22 years ago. He has been working with me ever since.

I often think of the comment made by an old farmer that, what my grandparents started would never last and they would soon be gone. But that was 69 years ago and we, their family, are still here. We continue the legacy of our truly heroic immigrant grandparents who were successful in defying all odds and obstacles.

*Top: Rosalie LaGates. Center: Joe and Julia Garavaglia, who opened Hill Top Inn, pose with daughter, Rosalie, in 1940. Bottom: Poster art of the Hill Top Inn, established in 1939 on Morganford.*

## TRICOLORED HOT-PEPPER APPETIZER

*This recipe came to light during Rosalie's visit to her hometown Inveruno and Legalo, suburbs of Milan in Lombardy. Rosalie, in top photo at left, also shows her marinated mushrooms, which are equally popular with her customers.*

| | |
|---|---|
| 2 yellow peppers | Thin pieces of ham |
| 2 orange peppers | Cheese |
| 2 red peppers | Olive oil |

Cut peppers in quarters lengthwise. Place in baking dish. Lay thin pieces of ham on the peppers, then some cheese. Sprinkle lightly with olive oil and bake in a pre-heated 350° oven until cheese melts.

### Francesca Gitto

With a sharp and detailed memory, the articulate and entertaining Francesca Gitto, 101 years old, fills the room with her laughter and inspires young people with stories of her adventures.

With sophistication and grace, Francesca is a talented artist who is always impeccably dressed. Growing up with 12 siblings, her life was filled with love despite all the hard times and poverty.

Whenever Francesca speaks of her own childhood, it is always with a sense of wonder and enthusiasm. "When we were children, we had to make our own fun. Toys were scarce, but we had a dog named Leo. My brother, Blaise, would hitch Leo up to our little wagon and we would all take turns riding around the neighborhood."

Mrs. Mugavero, Francesca's mother, taught herself how to read English which gave each of her children a love for reading. Francesca particularly enjoyed spending time in the library which was across the alley from St. Ambrose church.

"When I was a little girl, the original St. Ambrose church caught on fire. We were not allowed to leave class but we listened to the bells of the fire wagon, which was pulled by horses."

"My favorite memories are of my husband, George, a talented, handsome gentleman. I remember when he had to ask my father for permission to date me and, later, ask for my hand in marriage. God blessed us with three children, Paul, Charles, and George, Jr."

"George played the violin beautifully, actually making his own. Sometime on the telephone, he would play love songs to me. Sometimes this was embarrassing, because we had a party-line and all the neighbors could hear."

"As for now, life is good. I continue to read, crochet and I do enjoy playing bingo."

*In this circa-1910 photo, the family of Francesca Mugavero poses with their dog, Leo.*

*Francesca (Mugavero) Gitto, the mother of Charlie Gitto, Sr., at her First Communion. Her younger sister, Judy, stands on the stool at right.*

# OLD MEMORIES & OLD FRIENDS

### Arnoldo Denando

The character of an immigrant who built the Hill was exemplified in the early 1900s by Arnoldo Denando, a quiet gentle farmer in Italy. However, during World War I, he served in Italy's army but was captured by the Germans. As their prisoner, he was forced to work as a miner and to learn new skills which were strange to him, a farmer. An angry German officer beat him with the butt of his rifle, breaking his ribs. In dire pain, Denando was denied medical help. The government of Italy, after the war, awarded him a Medal of Honor.

John Tessaro, brother-in-law of Denando worked in the coal mines of Maryville in Southern Illinois. He convinced Denando to come. However, not having enough to pay passage for his wife, Mary, and children, John and Mary, for eight years he lived with his brother-in-law before he saved enough to bring over his family. Hearing about a new mine, Laclede Christy in St. Louis, he found a place for his family to live on the Hill and landed a job. However, mining was extremely hazardous: wooden planks barely protected against the roof caving in or miners could meet death through the dynamite explosions. After heavy rains, water was four feet deep in the mines. He often told his grandchildren about his work in the clay mine. "Sometimes we even dug the clay out by hand and piled it into the railcars. We were paid $1.00 for every car loaded."

Denando spoke of going often to Forest Park - not for picnics or pleasure, but to find materials left over from the World's Fair that could be used for building materials. He once carried home a railroad tie on his back to provide heat for his family.

But despite the dangers and difficulties he endured in mining, he spoke proudly of his work and thankful, there were no German soldiers beating him with a rifle in America.

*Photo Above: Pictured with Arnoldo are his grandchildren, Patricia and Lance. Photo Right: Arnoldo is flanked by Mr. and Mrs. Tessaro from Maryville in Southern Illinois.*

## Adriana Fazio

My parents were extraordinary. They came to America with my brother, Charlie, and my sister, Domenica, from Augusta, Sicily. My brother, Ben, and I were born in America. For many families, money was scarce. Fortunately, Mamma was a genius when it came to Sicilian pasta and sauces. Each night we savored a different pasta: pasta with peas, butter, basil; pasta with olive oil, garlic, fresh parsley, and Romano cheese; or a pasta with tomato sauce made with black olives, capers, and plenty of Parmesan cheese.

Sundays were different because the entire day was special. The best part was seeing my father, Ben Fazio, who was a baker and worked from the early evening until morning. He always slept during the day, except on Sunday, when we never left his side. After church, we came home and Mamma would

cook a delicious meal. I can still smell the aroma of bubbling tomato sauce, chunks of pork, beef sausages, and lots of fresh basil.

Summertime was also wonderful. We didn't have school, so Mamma would wake us up around 3:00 a.m. We would get dressed and Mamma would walk us over to the bakery to help Papa. When we finished working, Mamma took a loaf of warm, fresh bread, cut it lengthwise, drizzled olive oil on top, then sprinkled oregano over it. We would all sit on top of huge flour sacks, crunching that crusty loaf and savoring those moments.

Even as a child, I knew that one day I would cook Mamma's appetizing comfort food and Papa's heavenly bread. So much warmth–so much love. So, today my goal is to continue the legacy of my parents and fill my deli with that same warmth–special meals with special friends.

*Pictured below are Adriana's parents, Mr. and Mrs. Ben Fazio.*

*The girl in sixth grade, Adriana Fazio, no doubt voted Most Likely To Succeed, succeeded indeed. She later appeared on the Food Network with nationally known chef Mario Batali.*

## Louis Serra

Antonio P. Serra had the will and courage to leave his family to immigrate to America in 1906. Love was the catalyst which gave him the strength to work as a laborer in St. Louis, Missouri. It took seven difficult and lonely years for him to save enough money to send for his family. His dreams were realized when his wife, Rose, and their two children, Louis and Mary, arrived from Fuggia, Italy in 1913 aboard the ship *The Madonna*.

Rose was a talented seamstress who taught the trade to her daughter, Mary. They worked downtown at the Curlee Clothing Company, where her son, Louis, would eventually join them. After convincing them of the importance of education, Rose encouraged her son, Louis P. Serra, to attend classes in New Brunswick, Missouri so he could earn his certificate as a "state-registered" pharmacist. He became a successful pharmacist in the early years

of the Hill, later marrying Anna DiLiberta.

Louis' son, Joseph, remembers "I would dash out of St. Ambrose Church a little early in order to return to the drugstore so I could wait on customers after Mass."

Joseph continued to help his father even while attending Washington University School of Law. When Louis went home for dinner, Joseph served the Italian immigrants who spoke little English but brought along their children as translators.

"I was always amazed at the speed with which Italian immigrant children learned English," recalls Joseph. He also remembers the compassion of his kind-hearted father who would always say to him, "When you deliver medicine to our customers who live downtown in Little Italy, do not charge them for delivery–they shouldn't have to pay extra!"

After Louis' death, his wife, Anna, remodeled the drugstore, converting it into office space.

*Pictured in the Serra drugstore at 1935 Marconi, circa 1940s, are Jimmy LoPiccolo, Dr. Vincent LoPiccolo, Dr. Laudacina, and pharmacist, Louis Serra.*

*Above: In the 1940s, Jean Colombo Moore poses with her children David, Janet, and Leslie in this Christmas scene. Right: Born in Turbigo, Italy in 1922, Jean Colombo Moore poses with her sister, who later did not make the trip to America.*

## Jean Colombo Moore

Jean Colombo Moore was just a little eight-year-old when she and her family immigrated to America. She was a bright, curious child who was anxious to absorb every new sight.

When the family arrived in New York, they boarded a train to St. Louis where their relatives met them. Jean was in awe of Union Station. She said, "I had never seen anything like it in my whole life. It was like a castle and had so many lights. I could only think, 'I'm going to a great big city'"

What was new and strange to Jean was that her new home in America had two toilets, but they were not really bathrooms—just toilets. The bathtub was in the furnace room. She says, laughing, "In Italy, we had a well for water and the 'outhouse' was way off from the house." What captured her attention was that there was running water in the toilets. "This really intrigued me. My first night in America was spent running back and forth, flushing both toilets just to hear the running water!"

Knowing only the word "yes" in English, Jean was understandably apprehensive about starting school. It didn't take this bright little girl long before she learned to read and write in English. In 1931, she enrolled in Henry Shaw School and soon caught up with her classmates. She has always credited her patient teachers who encouraged her.

She recalls, "My mother never spoke English and my father worked hard. Like so many families, the Colombos were also poor and I could only go to high school for one year." Jean, however, was determined to get an education.

Looking back on her American adventure, she smiles as she observes, "I am so proud to be in America. Where in the world can a girl stop school when she was only 15, get a G.E.D. at sixty, and start college!"

*The Budweiser Clydesdales pay a surprise visit to Mike and Ida Carnaghi's Fairmount Tavern. Top: Mike poses inside his tavern.*

## Mike "The Milkman" Carnaghi

Labor is an extension of the personality of the immigrant. It is a way in which he defines himself as it measures his work and his humanity. Italian immigrants taught their children a strong work ethic so they could become somebody, because work meant more than acquisition of goods.

This is the lesson Mario (Mike) Carnaghi learned at an early age. Mario was born in Cuggiono, Italy in 1904. His parents settled in St. Louis' Hill section and he attended St. Ambrose School in 1909. Like so many children of immigrants, Mike left school after the third grade in order to help his family.

When he was only eight years old, Mike would walk along the railroad cars behind St. Ambrose Church carrying a huge burlap sack. His job was to gather up pieces of coal that had fallen from the train cars loaded with coal. Sometimes, older boys would jump on the cars and throw down coal so the younger children could fill up their sacks. It was in this way that he helped his family to survive the cold St. Louis winters.

As a young man, Mike courted and married lovely Ida Vago. He then became the Hill's "milkman" and, early each morning, he would hitch up his horse to a buggy and complete his route. As his business modernized, he drove a milk truck to make deliveries. Mike was known for his charity. He often cancelled bills for families who were unable to pay. After a large corporation bought his milk routes, Mike, the young son of immigrants, took another path along his journey. He purchased and managed Fairmount Tavern.

## Gino Mariani

### (As told by son, Eugene)

My father was a man true to his convictions. During his youth, he served in the Italian army from early 1918 to 1920. He fought against the Austrian forces in the closing of the First World War. When the war was over, he returned to his hometown, Valdottavo, near Lucca in Tuscany. Like many army veterans, he initially supported Mussolini. He once said, "In the beginning, I did what I could to help bring Mussolini to power. However, when I saw the tactics employed by him and the Fascists, I began to work against him."

As a leader in the local War Veteran's Association, my father was the guest speaker to unveil a monument in memory of men from Valdottavo who were killed in the war. In the town's main square, he praised the heroism of the soldiers and deliberately excluded mention of the Fascists. He was quickly labeled as an enemy of the party, which status forced him to flee the country. My father's family were labeled anti-Fascist. They were tortured *Il Purgativo* (Purification) when they were forced to drink castor oil to 'cleanse' their system.

My father had a difficult time entering the United States as there were quotas limiting the immigration of Italians. Through a family connection, he was certified as a journalist. His family bought him a round-trip, first-class steamship ticket from Genoa to New York. When he arrived, all immigrants had to pass through Ellis Island but, since my father was traveling as a journalist, he got the opportunity to bypass the red tape. When the ship docked, he simply walked off with the other first-class passengers. He was only 22 years old.

My father was a talented poet, scholar, and photographer. The Italian community has reaped rich rewards because my father had the courage to stand by his convictions, seeking freedom over tyranny.

*Gino Mariani is attired in the Second Bersalieri Roma uniform in 1918 on the occasion of a visit by President Wilson.*

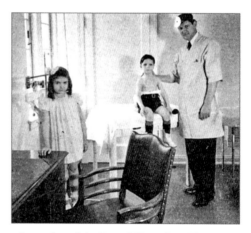

*The philosopher, poet, photographer, and longtime-Hill resident, Gino Mariani, takes a break from his creative endeavors.*

## Dr. Montani

"Medicine is not merely a science but an art. The character of the physician may act more powerfully upon the patient than the drugs employed."
–Paracelsus, circa 1525

The words of Paracelsus are certainly a valid description of Dr. Charles Montani who received his medical degree from St. Louis University Medical School in 1928. A son of Herrin, Illinois, Dr. Montani started his practice on the Hill. Paracelsus aptly describes Dr. Montani's character, personality, and dedication as they were exactly what the immigrant community needed. Gentle and caring, he treated each patient with special care.

From families who experienced the pangs of poverty, Dr. Montani would accept no money, not even allowing a discussion on the subject. No patient ever experienced the embarrassment of not being able to pay. He simply would not accept payment and he often said, "Put your money away, *Sposa*. I don't want it!" "*Sposa*" was what he would affectionately call any woman who came to his office. Meaning "Young Bride," they were all *Sposa* to him.

He never hesitated to make an emergency house call. In his mind, every call and every case called for immediate attention. One story relates a dash to a home after a mother's frantic call that her son was about to expire. Mary Cuchetti, the physician's nurse of many years, alerted Dr. Montani that the boy had a marble stuck in his nose. Mary also was frantic. Dr. Montani went directly to the home and extracted the marble, giving the boy a mild lecture for being so foolish.

Dr. Montani married and raised his family on the Hill, the neighborhood where he practised, and was admired and loved. It seems obvious that Paracelsus had someone like Dr. Charles Montani in mind when he wrote his memorable words.

*A member of the Sacred Heart Day Nursery School board, Dr. Charles Montani examines two young patients in 1942.*

*Leo Grillo taking passage to America.*

## Leo Grillo

"I was born in Licata, Sicily–one of five children to Salvatore Grillo and Angela Salviccio. When I was only three years old, my mother died at age 32. My father worked hard transporting produce throughout Licata.

In 1954, I left Sicily to find work. I stopped in Lisbon, Portugal and even met the exiled Prince of Italy. From Lisbon I went to Mexico. I couldn't find work there, so I decided to go to America. Within a year, I married my wife, Susanna Nicoletta.

My first job in America was waiting tables at the Chase Park Plaza. My father instilled in me a strong work ethic, so I took another job unloading trucks at night and later worked at an air conditioning factory during the day. Like so many Italians, I did not want to work for a 'padrone (boss),' so I started my own remodeling and construction company.

Arriving in America, I didn't know two words in English. But, I soon learned.

Now, I'm retired and just celebrated fifty-three of marriage to my beautiful wife. We have three good children (Linda, Anna, and Sal) and four grandchildren (Joseph, Michael, Stephanie, and Giovanna). I keep busy maintaining condominiums and a shopping center that I bought. Sometimes I look back and feel blessed to have the experiences of my life and then I think, "Not bad for a young immigrant! Only in America!"

*Leo Grillo, enduring wartime strife and a difficult childhood in Licata, Italy, returned in later years to a non-stop eating and drinking Italian festival.*

*Born in 1914, Ambrose Ranzini, who got a nickel for standing still for the picture, is at left with brothers, Frank, Martin, and Louis.*

## Ambrose Ranzini

In the 1920s, children of immigrants were often called upon to work under difficult circumstances to help support their families. Typical of this cultural phenomenon is the story told by longtime Hill resident, Ambrose Ranzini.

"In 1926, when I was only eleven years old, my brother, Frank, quit his job with our local baker, Mr. Carlo Baroli. But, no one called Carlo by his given name as he was simply known as "Reboon" because he came from the town of Rebone, Italy.

I could never understand why my brother would quit such a nice job. So, every Friday night, I reported to work, putting loaves in the proof box before being baked in the oven. The proof box is where the bread rises. Only then was I allowed to lie down on an old, bumpy cot so that I could rest for an hour or two. Then, very early Saturday morning, my job was to hitch the horse to the wagon and Reboon and I delivered bread to the homes on the Hill. Our last stop was at 5:00 a.m. Then, I took the horse back to unharness him. Finally, I could go home to sleep for two hours because at 8:00 a.m., we re-ran the route again for Sunday orders.

All the other bakeries were finished with Sunday orders by 10:00 a.m. on Saturday, but we never got home before 6:00 p.m. The reason was because at each stop, Reboon had a *cichet* (a shot glass of whiskey). He loved to chat or sing a tune or two while he enjoyed whatever liquor his customers offered him.

One very cold winter afternoon, I was outside shivering for two hours waiting for Reboon. But, I guess the horse was cold and tired too because he turned around and headed for the bakery. I decided to follow him, leaving Reboon behind.

The very next day, I told my mother that I quit! The worse part was that I didn't even earn a penny for all that effort in the freezing cold because Reboon had only paid me with BREAD!

# KNIGHTS IN DUSTY ARMOR

*Early Hill schoolboys, circa 1920s. Top row, standing: Louie Chiodini, Mike Crespi, Ben Sciuto, Ambrose Ranzini, Ted Ponciroli, Angelo Piatanida, and Charlie Fuse. Second row: Caesar Miriani, Emil Spezia, Louis Brusati, Frank Ranzini, and Angelo Oldani. First row: Johnny Oldani, Willie Merlo, Jasper Chiodini, Angelo Calcaterra, and Paul Garavaglia.*

*From a 1937 St. Louis Post-Dispatch article.*

When they were young men growing up on the Hill, they never claimed any title of distinction. Their domain was the corner of Macklind and Daggett Avenues. They were dubbed the "Alley Rats."

In 1928 the names claimed were: Steve and Mike Gioia; Lou, Lance, and Angelo (Jewlene) Berra; Raymond Riley; Caesar Airaghi; Frank (Master) Puricelli; John Garanzini; Arthur (Turro) Carnaghi; Mike (Marco) Pisani; Charles (Beef) Rolfi; Johnnie Garascia; Tino Colombo; Angelo Carnaghi; Angelo (Spasa) Colombo; Bob Demattei; Charlie (Utah) Garavaglia; Gus Colombo; Al and Jinx Whitmore.

The Alley Rats' days were rich with camaraderie and friendly capers. They did claim a private swimming area - the River Des Peres! Members only! Great for skinny-dipping.

The Alley Rats found an old horse which someone turned loose on Macklind field. Lew Berra said Jerry was so skinny "you could hang your coat on any bone that stuck out!" "We rode him bareback through Forest Park's Bridal Path right alongside of the rich people who wore riding pants and rode thoroughbreds!

In those days, Macklind field was one big hill. The Alley Rats initiated and completed the first baseball field. Using picks and shovels, they dug out an area for the field. "Then," remembered Lance, "we tied an old bed spring behind Jerry and we led him back and forth, dragging the spring and leveling out our diamond."

Ambitious, they earned money by going

## ALLEY RATS' THEME SONG
### to the tune of *Hinky Dinky Parlez Vous.*

*The Alley Rats went over the line,*

*Parlez Vous*

*The Alley Rats went over the line,*

*Parlez Vous.*

*The Alley Rats went over the line,*

*we're the happiest guys without a dime…*

*Hinky Dinky Parlez Vous!*

"Dump" hunting and selling lead and iron for scrap. "We used the extra money to go to the Highlands, the Macklind Theater, or the Family Theater. There used to be an outdoor theater where Spielberg's is today, and where Spielberg's warehouse is, there was the Scala Theater. It was owned by Angelo and Antoinette Colombo," reminisced Steve Gioia.

Catching cats for the local baker…marinating the cats in wine was another solid memory. They once caught an owl for Ribbone the Connoisseur.

The Alley Rats fondly remember Sergeant Wren, the stern but friendly and honest cop on the Hill. Sergeant Wren used to call the corner of Daggett and Macklind "The Barbary Coast." The Sergeant would stop and talk with the boys while he walked his beat.

If anyone needed help digging a basement, building a shed or constructing a fence, the Alley Rats were there to help. If a tree needed chopping, these bravados were there to help. They were truly Knights in Dusty Armor.

# HILL NICKNAMES

To quote Shakespeare: "What is in a name? That by any other name…" might well apply to any ethnic group. However, with Italians names are never so mundane, nor so simple. Rather, they each possess a quality of uniqueness.

Nicknames played a major role in the lives of the early Italian immigrants. They were considered *Soprannomi* (A name above a name) and were given in jest, affection, or acclaim. It seems the most ridiculous were the most adhesive and enduring. It is important to understand that while they may seem to outsiders to be less than complimentary, they were in the minds and hearts of members of the Hill community, terms of endearment.

The early Italian immigrant had a rather sad nickname for the first place they encountered in America. Ellis Island to them was *Isola della Lacrime* (Island of Tears)! It was duly named because many tears were shed there. To these brave immigrants it must have represented a place of sadness, and lonely exile from their homeland.

However, Hill nicknames were never so sad. They are more often humorous or even playful. They depict a mark of deeper intimacy and act as passports for friends. To be dubbed with a nickname made one an integral part of the community or as the Italians say *Un nome e un nome ma un soprannome e un dono!* (A name is a name, but a nickname is a gift!)"

There is no greater enjoyment than when friends get together and reminisce about the many various and often wild nicknames. With the mention of each, a story inevitably unfolds immediately producing much laughter. But always there is respect because it is good to look back, to remember, to smile, and to be proud.

Many have withstood the test of time. These are but a few of the Hill's recognized nicknames.

If you were to ask any old-timer on the Hill they would say to you *"Anere un soprannome alla montagna e simbolo di appartenza.* (To have a nickname on The Hill is a symbol of belonging.)"

## Laudy
While growing up on the Hill, the famous Yankee catcher was never referred to as "Yogi." His given name was Lawrence and his mother in her fractured English called him Laudy for Lawrence. His nickname was picked up by his friends when they heard his mother calling out "Laudy come home!"

## Flash
Joseph Caputa did his work slowly and deliberately. He was quite a perfectionist. His friends named him Flash, the opposite of his demeanor, as is often the case. His younger brother Frank inherited his title.

## Muscles
As a youngster, Tony Labarbera was very thin and had a slight build. His friends good-naturedly called him Muscles!

## Papa Probst
It was not often that non-Italians bestowed a nickname on a member of the Hill community. But way back when the Hill still had many German residents, Frank Gianella was the proud owner of a neighborhood tavern and many of the patrons were Germans. Whenever his little son would run into the tavern calling "Papa, Papa!" the men would hold up their steins and shout "Probst!" and so for many years the tavern became known as Papa Probst.

## Joe Budlajo
Joseph Pozzoli was never happier than when he walked home after a stint at a local tavern. Rather than walk, he more often stumbled, which earned him the name Joe Budlajo...loosely translated as "Joe Fall Down."

## Biggie
Julius Garagnani was known to try things in a big way– hence the nickname. An adventurous entrepreneur, he opened a restaurant named Stan Musial and Biggie's with baseball great, Stan Musial.

## Midge
As a child, Louis Berra was short and slight, thus his friends called him "midget." He not only grew in stature, he also grew to be the Hill's beloved politician. However, everyone lifelong referred to him as Midge Berra.

# ROSE'S TAVERN

Anna Jo Hof remembers her grandparents in the following memoir.

In the early 1900s my grandparents, Giuseppe and Maria Spezia, immigrated to America. My grandfather was determined to be his own boss, so he purchased a two-story building on Edwards on the Hill which housed a tavern on the first floor and two apartments above.

My grandparents had one child, Rose, who was born in 1911. Rose, my mother, often spoke of Spezia's Tavern. They served draft beer, soda, and ice cream. The tavern was crowded with children choosing one of Grandpa's three scoops at 3 different prices - 2 cents, 5 and 10 cents!

Every evening most of the surrounding families sent their children to the saloon to get a bucket of draft beer which was placed on the table for all to drink with dinner. Grandpa believed that every true Italian must have his own vines for grapes and wine. He planted a grape-

vine patio which was enjoyed by many over the years. Grandpa also had a three-room house built next to the saloon where, during Prohibition, liquor, beer, and wine were sold from the basement. In 1931, my mother married Charles Grassi and they moved into that little house. It was there that I was born in 1937, delivered by Hill midwife, Maria Volpe.

When Grandpa Giuseppe became ill my mother and father bought the saloon. The name then changed from Spezia's to Charlie's Place. It continued to be a very friendly and family-oriented tavern. During this era, bocce courts were added. When the older, retired men were at the saloon, it would be difficult to judge who yelled the loudest, the bocce players or the men who played Italian card games called *mariana* and *scoppa*.

In 1953, my Dad died and my Mom and John Puricelli, my dad's former partner, ran the business and it continued to thrive. It re-

mained a place for families to enjoy Grandpa's grape arbor and watch bocce. Barbeques were held and bocce trophies were awarded.

In 1971, the third generation, my husband, Tom, and I took over and the Spezia's of the early 1900s took on a modern look. A new bocce court with a roof allowed the game to be played in all kinds of weather. We enlarged the grape arbor and put in concrete tables, which made a charming and inviting patio. In 1979, Tom and I sold the business which is currently home to Lorenzo's Trattoria.

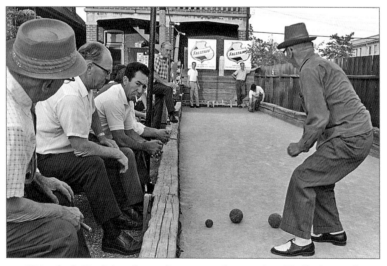

*Using body English, a bocce player coaxes his team's red balls close to the pallino. Bocce was played at Rose's Tavern from 1930 to 1980.*

*Friends meet at Rose's Tavern, where Rose's husband, Charlie Grasso, tends bar.*

# ALDO DELLA CROCE

It has been said that a work of art is the unique result of a unique temperament. Its beauty comes from the fact that the artist is what he is. These words certainly describe Aldo Della Croce, whose character reflects honesty, gentleness, and humility. It is in his works of art that we see strength, yet a softness of beauty.

One's own environment often brings forward talent which may otherwise lie dormant. Aldo's early years were spent in a little village in Tuscany, called Bagni di Lucca. He was surrounded by the richness and artistic beauty of his historical hometown with surrounding walls perfectly preserved throughout time. Filled with pride Aldo spoke of Lucca, "From my town I could see the mountains. They were magnificent. I could almost feel the presence of our great God who made them!" He also remembered the mineral spring waters nearby as odorless and rich in bicarbonate and calcium. It was not uncommon to see foreigners of all nationalities come to enjoy thermal treatments in the Lucca waters, which were considered to have healing powers. Among the visitors were renowned poets, writers, and artists. Aldo smiled as he recounted what a reporter once said referring to the many members of Europe's aristocracy visiting the Bagni di Lucca: "*Ai Bagni di Lucca si sta fra altezze reali fino a mezza gamba!* (In Bagni di Lucca, one is knee deep in royal highnesses!)"

But, below the mountains in his village, Aldo spent his days going to school and enjoying his family's parish church, San Pietro. "My church is 1300 years old," he relates. "Tuscany holds on to old, beautiful churches. Today, countries are too quick to tear them down."

Most of the townspeople were artisans sculpting figures from Plaster of Paris. They sold their work throughout Europe.

As a young boy, Aldo sculpted and fashioned figures. He never formally studied art as this gift came naturally. His own father worked on statues as a side job primarily to better support his wife and seven children. Living so close to many artisans, and in an area so rich culturally, awakened Aldo's senses to artistic beauty.

"I learned a lot by watching the men practicing their trade, working with simple tools."

Perhaps that's why Aldo had no need for fine tools. It is more likely because his art was not in his tools, nor in his hands, but in his heart.

When Aldo grew to be a young man he worked in a little shop in Lucca. It was there that Aldo fell in love with and married lovely Assunta. They were blessed with a beautiful daughter, Danielle.

Aldo remembers, "In 1958, we left my beautiful Tuscany and immigrated to America, where I plied my trade in Assunta's father's business, Figure Craft located in St. Louis."

Aldo's work became more intense and vibrant with the use of his special glazes and antiquating patterns. His creations are definitely the result of his unique temperament. He sought perfection in his work and spent tireless hours until he reached his goal. "Each piece of sculpture," he asserts, "must always be better than the last. An artist should never be satisfied with anything less than excellence."

He believes that nothing can come out of an artist that is not in the man. It can truly be said the beauty of Aldo's art reflects Aldo the man - honest, gentle, humble, and talented.

*Aldo Della Croce from Lucca, Italy, learned how to sculpt from his sculptor father then, after he and his wife, Assunta, came to America, he worked with his father-in-law who owned Figure Craft in St. Louis.*

*The Hawk's Clubhouse, was one of the 25 Hill athletic clubs, providing safe and wholesome youth activities. Most were under the guidance of Uncle Joe Causino.*

# UNCLE JOE CAUSINO

The man who was to direct the Hill's athletic fortunes arrived in 1925. Joseph Causino walked into St. Ambrose Church, eager to proselytize sport and brotherhood. Joe represented a new breed of social worker formally trained as a recreation director and was employed by the St. Louis South Side YMCA.

Most Italo-Americans viewed sport as a means of supporting the dignity of a group as well as providing communal pride. Representing a socially approved safety valve, sports generated a galaxy of local and national role models, which provided an excellent and effective dialogue with the rest of St. Louis. Uncle Joe's program served as the facilitator.

Uncle Joe's school ran like a game of football with many huddles, scrimmages, and rap sessions. But the end-result was like a well-run playbook producing many graduates who represented proud icons of Italian-American strength and dignity. Phil Verga was one of the men who attested to Causino's decisive impact on his life. "Uncle Joe was dynamite! If you needed dough, he gave you money. If

you needed a job, he'd help you find one." Les Garanzini concurred: "He was concerned with us kids on the Hill. He got us sponsors for each club…ours was the Fawns…then he had this clubhouse – he'd let us use it. We also got to go camping and hiking." Whenever the boys got out of line or got smart, Uncle Joe took them by the ear. Most importantly, he used to let the Hill clubs play and swim at the YMCA, even though the boys were not members nor could afford the membership. For kids who normally played on the streets, that was a real treat. Moreover, Joe's wife was well respected for keeping the girls in line and out of trouble, especially in regard to the boyfriend situation.

Uncle Joe's sense of morality, fairness, and team pride must have worked because the rate of delinquency decreased on the Hill with this man's arrival. In 1949, a St. Louis columnist rhapsodized that "…all is not spaghetti, macaroni and choice wine on the Hill, that famed neighborhood in Southwest St. Louis. The principal occupation is sports and the main export nationally is known athletes. Many

people think that it is baseball…but almost every other sport has produced a similar quota of great stars." In 1951, the *Post-Dispatch* admired the fact that the Hill was comprised of some 12,000 first- and second-generation Italians that boasted its own factories, stores, schools and churches. "But best of all, it boasts of being a neighborhood with the lowest juvenile delinquency rate in the city."

Mickey Garagiola did not mince any words to explain why there were so few law-breakers on the Hill. "Juvenile delinquency. No way. If we didn't watch ourselves, our dads would beat our tails. And if they didn't, Joe would tan our hides. And if Uncle Joe missed us, the priests would haul us in the rectory for a conference. Stay out till eleven and you saw the priest."

So it wasn't just Uncle Joe but the support of diligent parents and the overseeing concern of the Church that helped to keep young people out of jail and out of trouble to uphold the family's good name. The latter has always been integral to a community like the Hill.

# FATHER KOESTER

Charles Koester, a young seminarian, studied for the priesthood at the North America College in Rome. Unfortunately, his studies were interrupted because of Italy's entrance into World War II. He returned to the U.S. and was ordained a priest in December 1940.

Fortunately for the Hill community, Rev. Koester was appointed to serve St. Ambrose Parish in March of 1942. He was loved by everyone because of his genuine kindness and care for each parishioner. When he started his mission, the United States was at war. More than 750 sons from the Hill had left their homes to fight for America.

Father Koester knew he had to do something special to support these brave young men. Speaking to members of the Crusader Club, he encouraged them to help publish a newsletter letting the servicemen know what was going on in the neighborhood and how to contact others serving their country!

In no time, the Crusaders collected addresses and met to work in the St. Ambrose rectory. Quinn Garavaglia still jokes that "Monsignor Lupo was in control of the heat that winter so we never took our coats off. Father was the proofreader and he even borrowed a mimeograph machine and in no time *The Clarion* was ready to be sent out." Nine young ladies dubbed "The Crusader Slave Gang" (CSG) by Father Koester took on the role of mailing. *The Clarion* was sent all over the world. Hill boys fighting for America began sending letters to Father Koester telling of their experiences. Segments of their letters were published so that others could share news. It proved a great morale builder.

Another reason that Father Koester was popular is that he would let some of the young men back home borrow his Green Hornet vehicle to go to the Highland's dance hall in Forest Park every Saturday night. And when the Green Hornet came down the street at 10:30 p.m. the gossip was out that the Father had been out late at night.

After the war *The Clarion* was continued as a neighborhood newsletter with the original editorial staff: Father Koester, Angelo Pastori, Anthony Quinn Garavaglia, Angeline Mazzola, and Mary (Monti) Traina.

Father Koester was transferred to St. Laborius in November 1950 and the last issue was published.

He had other missions but he often said: "I have a special place in my heart for the people on the Hill." When it was announced that he was to become a bishop, one of his friends called him and said; "Yes, there is a God." And friends on the Hill are grateful to Him for sending Bishop Koester to be a blessing to many.

*Father Koester in his Green Hornet.*

*Father Koester appears with his church staff.*

*Pictured are the nine young ladies dubbed "The Crusader Slave Gang," (CSG) who helped Father Koester publish* The Clarion.

61

# FRANK BORGHI

Frank Borghi is recognized as a hero of the 1950s World Cup Soccer game. In Belo Horizonte, Brazil, 70,000 fans cheered him screaming, "Magnifico." That day, Frank became America's sports' hero when the U.S. team edged out the heavily favored England team by a score of 1-0. The British were constantly thwarted by Frank, the star goalkeeper.

It was during England's chance at a penalty kick that Frank made a brilliant save and literally won the game. He was carried off the field on the shoulders of wildly cheering spectators. Frank will modestly say, "I remember being frightened when all those fans began rushing toward me at the whistle. I was looking around for a place to hide. What I didn't realize was they just wanted to honor us."

Frank was truly a hero in the battlefield of athletics, but few know that he also was heroic on the fierce battlefield of war.

Over 65 years ago, Frank Borghi, only 18 years old, was drafted in the Army. He served as a medic in five major campaigns in the European Theatre. At 19, he was caring for soldiers wounded in battle. Yet, Frank will always say, "The heroes are the guys we left behind and those in the Veteran's Hospital. God was on my side and I was a lucky G.I.!"

With a look of sadness, Frank reminisced, "I remember the Hedge Row campaign in Normandy. One day I came across a wounded German soldier lying in a gully. He had a shrapnel wound in his chest. I administered sulphur crystals in his wound to prevent infection."

"I'll always remember how he looked at me with sincere gratitude. Before I left him I took off my raincoat and covered him."

"I became very good friends with a soldier we called 'Slim' Le Bar. When it was cold we would dig a very large trench for sleeping. One day Slim saw a soldier coming behind me ready to shoot. Slim shot him in the forehead and saved my life. We still keep in touch."

Something that many do not know about this sports figure and war hero is that Frank quit school to help support his mother after the death of his father. He worked at Famous & Barr Co. Frank would jump off the back of a truck to make deliveries for the merchandiser. He also worked at his uncle's funeral home where he offered care and kindness to grieving families.

Frank considers one of his greatest blessings are the friends he has kept since the days they were members of the Ravens Club. "We have been together since age 14 and we are closer than brothers," he relates. Even today they continue to meet once a week for lunch.

But it is safe to say that his love for his beautiful wife, Rosemarie, and his children made him their greatest hero. Rosemarie lovingly remembers, "When Frank would turn the corner coming home from work. All seven children dashed out to meet and throw their arms around him."

So today there is little physical athletics, the war is over, and some friends are gone. But Frank's family, his lovely Ro, his grown children continue to tell the world he is their hero!

*St. Ambrose boy's team, front row photo center, features a future world champion goalkeeper, Frank Borghi.*

*During World War II, Frank Borghi was a medic who saved the life of sports announcer, Jack Buck.*

*Frank Borghi sits with the man whose life he saved in the Battle for the Bridge of Remagen 50 years earlier. Also in the photo is Joe Torre, manager of the Cardinals, from 1990 to 1995.*

# JACK BUCK "ON THE HILL"

*From an interview with Beverly Buck Brennan*

Living on the Hill was so satisfying an experience for the family of Jack Buck, the eleventh announcer inducted into the Broadcaster's Wing of the Baseball Hall of Fame in 1987, that daughter Christine Buck once said she thought their surname was short for "Buckarelli."

In 1954, Jack and Alyce, 'unloaded' at 5405 Elizabeth with Jack Jr., Christine, Betsy, Grandma Buck, two turtles and a parakeet named 'Bucky.' Elizabeth was already a street paved with the notoriety of Joe Garagiola and Yogi Berra. It was about to produce another.

Jack Buck came from Columbus, Ohio to work for St. Louis Cardinals' General Manager Bing Devine. For almost the next half century, Jack's niche and his lifelong passion remained his family, St. Louis, and the Cardinals. According to his daughter, Beverly Buck Brennan, her dad was a multi-talented yet humble and contented man, who, unlike many of his stature, never hired an agent to "improve his stature in the entertainment industry." The Hill was also a niche, which suited the Buck family and created a cornucopia of memories.

The school-aged Buck children were enrolled at Shaw School though most of their friends attended St. Ambrose. Alyce Buck was a strong proponent of public education but that didn't stop the family from embracing everyone they encountered on the Hill. Beverly Buck Brennan reminisced, "I used to walk to school with my friend Jeanie Colombo, had a grade school crush on Stephen Tommania and my girlfriends were Rose and Carmen DiGregorio, Jimmy Garavaglia, Veronica Balazina and Debbie Puricelli." Alyce was very close with the next-door Garavaglias who often hosted the family to dinner.

Beverly also remembers: Opening gifts of sleds and bikes from Hanneke's Hardware on Christmas Day; Running and giggling, clad only in their underwear or morning pajamas to buy popsicles and penny candy from Angelo Oldani's; Singing and dancing in costumes at the annual pageant at Shaw Park.

Beverly recalls the many wonderful dinners and friendships with restaurateurs: "One of our favorite family evenings on Muny nights was dinner at Ruggeri's. We still have fond memories of Mickey Garagiola serving dad his lifelong favorite, spaghetti and meatballs. He enjoyed that here and at Cunetto's, having a close friendship with the Cunetto brothers.

According to Beverly, there was plenty of excitement that caused mom and dad concern. "I remember one day when Sam DiGregorio brought over two Clydesdales from Anheuser-Busch into our backyard. A swarm of bees attacked, I screamed and the two horses bolted with Christine and me hanging on for dear life. We smashed through trees and clotheslines. I lost two teeth. Christine's injuries sent her into a coma for several days as my anguished parents kept constant vigil by her bedside." Thankfully, Christine recovered but that event was also embroidered into the patchwork of life on the Hill for the Buck family.

Nevertheless, on June 2nd, 2003, the day the 5400 block of Elizabeth Avenue was renamed The Hall of Fame Place in honor of Yogi Berra, Joe Garagiola, and their legendary Cardinals' broadcasting father, Christine Buck received due applause when she proclaimed the Hill "the best neighborhood to grow up in."

*A Buck birthday on Elizabeth Avenue. Beverly Buck holds the cake for little Jack on the occasion of his fourth birthday in 1955. Christine Buck, on the right, holds on to one of her brother's new toys.*

*One month before relocating to St. Louis, Jack Buck is photographed next to his 1954 blue Plymouth, one of his all-time favorite cars, according to his daughter, Beverly Buck Brennan.*

# MEMORIES OF NONNIE

Old photos are a gift, images speaking to us from generations past. It is easy to lose oneself while staring into the eyes of our ancestors, contemplating what their lives were like forty, fifty, or a hundred years ago. It is a privilege to be the recipient of these historical records as they give us much more than stagnant likeness. They are a brief glimpse into our loved ones' daily lives.

A much-loved favorite is of a young girl; age thirteen posing for her first photograph (See Page 2 Book Dedication photo). Maria Anna Alberti, Marietta to her family, had just arrived in America, making the daring journey alone. She was called to her journey by her father, Carlo, who, one by one, wanted to bring his family to this new land of opportunity. She was put on the ship *Prinzess Irene* in Genoa and arrived in New York on October 14, 1903.

When staring into the eyes of this young girl in the photo, one wonders what were her thoughts on board this ship? Was she excited or scared, sick from the crossing, or worried about finding her way alone from New York to Saint Louis? In the picture, you only see a teenager in a wrinkled shirtwaist dress, trying to look grown-up with her hair piled atop her head Gibson style. A brooch is pinned to her high neck collar and she casually holds a fresh flower. Who is this courageous girl, half smiling at the camera. What became of her?

She was met at St. Louis Union Station by her sisters, five ambitious, forward-thinking women, who hid from her and popped out one by one to surprise the frightened Marietta who thought they had forgotten her. The Alberti sisters had married and made lives for themselves in Saint Louis before their baby sister joined them. However, they all worked, owned and ran businesses here. Marietta worked at one of their enterprises—a bar/boarding house known as The Rock House on the riverfront. She worked for her sister, cooking and cleaning, but also relaxing and enjoying the weekend dances that were held at the establishment. It was here at one of the dances that Marietta met and fell in love with Angelo Berra, marrying him at the tender age of sixteen.

Not all heroes discover new lands, write legislature, invent devices, or start a business. Some are heroic in their everyday life, the heroic deeds of living, loving, and raising a strong, united family. Marietta Berra is just such a hero. She bravely survived being a young mother whose first born son died of diphtheria before his second birthday. She buried her son and valiantly carried on to bear and raise nine more children. She worked hard and kept her family together through illnesses, hardship, and the untimely death of her husband, Angelo. Marietta taught herself to read and write English and demanded that her husband and children speak English "like Americans." It was this young girl, unable to complete her own education, who instilled a love of learning in her children and subsequent generations. She read the newspaper daily, always found time to read her prayer book, and encouraged her family to read and "know new things."

The greatest gift this quiet hero left her clan was a love of family. She would not stand for infighting among her children. When tempers flared, as was normal in a household of nine gregarious children, she would end the disruptions with a simple look from her darting hazel eyes, a 'tsk' of her tongue, and say, "That is your brother; your brother always." The unity she formed in her brood translated to the next generation—twelve grandchildren that she would proudly say were all educated professionals. She forged our camaraderie and friendships around her dining room table every Sunday. How simple it is to take for granted the love we were able to share weekly. While growing up, the twelve of us just assumed that everyone did this. Marietta, now 'Nonnie' to her grandchildren, would cook all morning; making risotto, a roast, salad, fresh vegetables, and desserts. When the afternoon came, her children, their spouses, and families would gather around the sturdy oak table in the immense kitchen, now dwarfed with the number of people crammed into it. At Nonnie's dinner she insisted, "No, no, no. No children's table—we all eat together. We only eat as one." As a child, I could never understand her reluctance to let us spread out into other rooms. I now know that this was her way of keeping us together physically and, more importantly, emotionally.

It is the precious gift of family that she gave us. We now live all across the country, and two more generations of the Berra Clan have been born. However, no matter how far apart we are or how much time passes between us, our bond is deep. Our love was nurtured and nourished by Nonnie, the young girl in the photograph. When we are together now, we reminisce about her, our parents, aunts, uncles, and the unique events of our childhood. There is nothing better than sitting back at one such occasion and looking at the tables and tables of bloodline that came from Marietta, all laughing, loving, and enjoying nothing better than being together.

— Story by Eleanore Berra Marfisi about her mother, Maria Anna Alberti.

# A History of Italian Restaurants
## IN ST. LOUIS, MISSOURI

It is hard to believe but the Hill, circa 1930, boasted a single restaurant, Sala's. There were 21 confectioneries, 19 grocers, 13 saloons, and 9 barber shops. While the immigrated Italians enjoyed an icy gelato, a fresh-baked cannoli or imbibed coffee, wine or beer, they did not eat outside the family domain. By the time 1940 arrived, only a handful of restaurants and lunchrooms had thrown open their doors on the Hill, perhaps as a form of testing ground. Most of these were located on Kingshighway or Manchester Boulevard, which indicated they played safe by catering to an American customer base. In reality, few Italians arriving on U.S. soil could afford the luxury of dining out and savory Italian cooking had yet to gain a reputation as well as toehold in the hearts and stomachs of the masses.

*By the year 1959, the Manno family with its five sisters, four of which had married John Mineo, Agostino Gabriele, Giovanni Gabriele, Franco Sanfilippo, had settled in America along with Mamma Elena and Papa Paul Manno. Son Paul Manno had immigrated earlier. Some of the finest dining establishments in St. Louis were spawned from these sisters, their husbands, and their offspring. The photograph captures a farewell–leaving Palermo for America.*

One of those that did get an early toehold was Sala's. Angelo Sala learned the culinary craft in Italy at the Ristorante di Sala under the tutelage of his war-hero (Garibaldi's Red Shirts) uncle, Antonio. Arriving in America in 1904, Angelo hauled sewer tile in St. Louis but held onto his dream and finally earned enough to open a saloon at South Kingshighway and Daggett in 1911. Around 1914, a typical saloon included a free-lunch table. Soon the lunches grew as popular as the pails the children carried from there to their fathers at the end of each working day. Angelo founded a café soon thereafter, operating it with his wife, Emma, until 1945 when they retired and left it to their seven children. The café survived Prohibition, the Depression, the war years, and even the construction of a viaduct in 1937 that shadowed it. It had been known for its sandwiches, steaks, and pasta. It was busiest in World War II, when at times it operated 23 hours a day serving around-the-clock shifts of

workers at nearby businesses converted to war plants. The family - minus the four sons then in military service - lived above the restaurant in the Hill neighborhood. Sala's was a south St. Louis landmark for 65 years.

In the 1930s, most of the Sala clientele were from the city's Southside German neighborhood. Not Italians. "The immigrant Italians came to my back door to work, not eat out," explained Angelo. Since the patriarchal German male indulged himself inside the eatery while wives and daughters waited outside in the car, the Salas hit upon a novel idea: curb side service for women.

Future restaurateurs like Angelo and Carmen Lombardo and Charlie Gitto, Sr., while in high school, re-

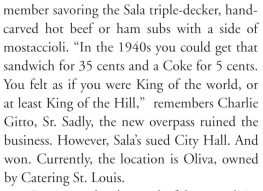

member savoring the Sala triple-decker, hand-carved hot beef or ham subs with a side of mostaccioli. "In the 1940s you could get that sandwich for 35 cents and a Coke for 5 cents. You felt as if you were King of the world, or at least King of the Hill," remembers Charlie Gitto, Sr. Sadly, the new overpass ruined the business. However, Sala's sued City Hall. And won. Currently, the location is Oliva, owned by Catering St. Louis.

But it was also those colorful personalities who ran restaurants or those who frequented

*Above: Arriving in America in 1904, Angelo Sala in 1911 opened a typical saloon, which included a free-lunch table. He founded a café (photo right, before the viaduct over it was built) soon thereafter and operated it with his wife, Emma, until 1945, when his children took over. Sala's was located on the corner of Kingshighway and Daggett.*

them that played a large part in their longevity and kept locals coming back for more.

What became Cunetto's, the old Brass Key, used to have a reputation for failed enterprises. Except for the fact that it was the place where Midge Berra, longtime South St Louis political force, held court during the 1950s and early 1960s. He was the kind who, if you had a problem, he could get it fixed for you downtown. He could be seen at the Brass Key on most days. After sitting down, citizens of the Hill waited patiently to share their problems and concerns with Midge.

The Brass Key Tavern was later taken over by Julius "Biggie" Garagnani and Charlie Ray. During the 1940s and 1950s, Saturday was a special night to hang out even though it was considered a bar, and no food was served. The name was changed to Rigoletto's up until those very personable and efficient Cunetto brothers took over. Pharmacists by trade, they also had a golden touch when it came to eateries. It didn't take long for Cunetto's to garner a following and then keep its flame alive for many generations to come.

In 1945, with the return of the veterans from World War II, the 'ristorante' enjoyed a sudden rise in popularity. This was mainly because many a hungry soldier had savored the delicious fare while seated at a family trattoria far away from home. America underwent a surge of affluence. Add to that mix, singers such as Perry Como, Frank Sinatra, and Dean Martin. They melodically connected good, Italian food to *amore* and taverns and soda parlors evolved into full-service eateries.

About this time, there were only four restaurants on the Hill: Ruggeri's, Sala's down the block on Daggett, Paul Berra's (later Rigazzi's, also on Daggett) and Oldani's run by Lou 'Spotty' Oldani. Spotty (whose nickname is due to a bald spot which resulted from a car hitting his bicycle) was a former drummer. At age 26, when his father passed away in 1932, he converted his father's tavern into a restaurant, dressing up the place with a canopy from the curb to the front door. Overstuffed chairs in the lounge allowed patrons to relax and enjoy Spotty's company while waiting to dine. Ravioli, made from both pork and beef, along with the steak and lobster menu kept his patrons coming back for more. In 1960, Oldani's was sold and the location later became Mama Campisi's. At age 96, and a 64-year resident of Ladue, Spotty remains an engaging conversationalist.

Anyone, including movie stars, flush with cash, patronized Ruggeri's at the corner of Edwards and Elizabeth. The steaks were charcoalsizzled in the basement and many residents can still smell the tantalizing aroma of steak and fresh garlic wafting over the Hill.

Also on Shaw, there was Angelo's, run by Louise and Angelo Oldani, which is the current Charlie Gitto's "On the Hill." Charlie Gitto, Sr. was once the maitre d' of Angelo's

*When Rose's restaurant was razed in Little Italy to make way for the St. Louis Convention Center, Rose's chef of 20 years, Giuseppe (Joseph) Pugliese, purchased the equipment and fixtures and opened Giuseppe's (photo left).*

*Photo right: Antonia and Giuseppe Pugliese. In 1973, starting off as a four-table restaurant at the old Chex Grill at Grand and Meramec, the Pugliese family began serving pizza, signature meatballs, and Italian specialties. There were multiple expansions in the 1980s and 1990s. The elite restaurateurs in town used to frequent Giuseppe's of a Sunday, a great compliment to "Mr. Joe."*

and Charlie, Jr. would work after school cleaning behind the bar, polishing the brass, and earning 75¢ a day. In 1981, Charlie, Jr. purchased the building from Angelo's three sisters: Gina, Mary, and Teresa. He later added a garden room, remodeled the kitchen, and expanded the dining area.

However, what was dining out Italian-style during the 1940s and 1950s for the common man on the Hill? On a Friday night he lined up at Berra's walk-up window to buy a pound or half a pound of fried fish. The breadwinner brought it home and his wife added a homemade spaghetti and salad. Berra's Café, besides fish, was known for its beef sandwiches, plate lunches, and ravioli. Sala's, Augusti's, and Milo's (the old Wil-Mar Lounge) also had takeout windows and sold good amounts of old-school fried cod, whitefish, perch, or jack salmon.

Charlie Gitto Sr., owner of Charlie Gitto's Downtown, has fond memories of the famed Cassani's eatery back in those good 'ole days. Mike Cassani, whose grandfather came from Italy in the 1880s, lived with his parents above their restaurant, Cassani's Café. Mike and Ann Cassani ran the place on Daggett and Hereford while Annie Bartoni cooked their signature barbecue ribs in the back kitchen. "I ate there every day in the 8th grade in the 1940s with the working folk from the Hill and the city," recalls Charlie. "You got a hamburger for 35¢, a beef plate lunch with mashed potatoes for 45¢, and a piece of pie and a Coke for a nickel each." This restaurant also catered to employees from Quick-Meal, which made Magic Chef stoves in the neighborhood. In the late 1950s,

*Cafferata's Café, photographed in 1915, has a line of jitneys dropping off customers to this fine dining establishment. The photo is captured on Delmar Boulevard, looking west to Taylor.*

Anne Cassani sold the restaurant to John and Marie Galimberti. This café was remembered for its Thursday night steam tables where two servers carved up beef, ham on-the-bone, or corned beef. Fridays offered great macaroni and cheese and, on the weekends, the aroma of barbecue filled the neighborhood as John manned the barbecue pits out back.

Andreino DeSantis, newly-arrived restaurateur from Italy, was an innovator on the Hill, who broke the old-country mold of "red spaghetti sauce" at his restaurant, Andreino's (later Dominic's). Richard Ronzio worked there as a bartender and Charlie Mugavero served as its maitre d'. Together this famous duo opened first a deli in University City in the late 1960s, then a trattoria near the old Arena on Oakland: hence the beginning of the Rich & Charlie's enterprise and the spin-off Pasta House Co.

Angelo Pastori had worked as part owner of the original Pastori's Restaurant on Laclede Avenue. In 1966, with his wife, Julia, he established Pastori's West at the intersection of Macklind and Daggett, the current home of Gian-Tony's on the Hill. Many remember enjoying family entertainment like Santa Claus parties along with the pony and cart rides.

Moving away from the Hill into Little Italy downtown, Charlie Gitto, Sr. recalls, "I worked at Al's Steak House when I was 17 years old. The place did a great business on Saturday night as a cafeteria at First and Biddle. I always remember the owner, Mrs. Barroni, saying, 'People have to leave with a good taste, whether from a great cup of coffee or dinner at a good price.' She was right and many res-

*Cicardi's, like Garavelli's, was also a five-star restaurant, located on the corner of Euclid and Delmar in the West End. On par with the best hotel dining rooms during the 1910s and 1920s, its building and interior was featured in* Missouri's Contribution to American Architecture (1928). *The edifice was built in 1914 and torn down in 1925 to make room for the Roosevelt Hotel.*
*Photos both pages courtesy of the Missouri History Museum-Library and Research Center*

Joseph Garavelli opened a restaurant on the corner of DeBaliviere and De Giverville. "One of the most beautiful restaurants in St. Louis, a national institution, known the length and breadth of the nation and employing more than 200 persons, mostly of Italian extraction and serving an average of 3,000 people a day."

At one time, Garavelli's Restaurant and Fountain Room also featured small trees and fountains with exotic birds, gorgeous red and green pheasants, and beautiful parakeets. They all contributed to make Garavelli's "an artistic jewel" that was designed in pure Italian style by Angelo Corrubia.

taurants in St. Louis rose or fell because of that little philosophy."

One of those that rose was a place in Little Italy called Rose's, which started as Rosario's Restaurant on 10th and Franklin in 1927. The place introduced the original southern Italian fresh cooking style to St. Louis. In 1933, Jasper Bonaventure purchased the restaurant and changed the name to Rose's, in honor of his wife. During his ownership, Rose's became one of downtown St. Louis' premier meeting spots. In the 1930s and 1940s, Washington Avenue was the clothing, fur, hat and shoe center of the Midwest, and many customers of those industries were taken to Rose's for dinner. In the late 1940s, downtown St. Louis was known for late-night restaurants. Rose's became a favorite after an evening aboard the *Admiral*. On any given Saturday night it would not be unusual to see a long line outside the door at 2:00 am.

Giuseppe (Joseph) Pugliese had been a chef at Rose's since he came to America in 1957. In 1973, Rose's traditional recipes almost disappeared when it was razed to make way for the St. Louis Convention Center. Fortunately, "Mr. Joe" purchased the equipment and fixtures from Rose's to continue the tradition. He rented the old Chex Grill at Grand and Meramec and opened a 4-table restaurant. The irresistible pizza and carry-out Italian food went over great especially in the 1980s with the Cardinal players. When Joe Torre first went to the Mets in 1995, he would come back into St. Louis and dine at Giuseppe's. "Mr. Joe" would make sure that the Mets' manager always had a fresh fruit platter for Torre's late-night dining.

A great compliment to Giuseppe's was, during the 1980s and 1990s when the elite restaurant families, Vince and Tony Bommaritos, Favazzas, the Cunettos, Amighettis, Gabrieles, Del Pietros, Mannos, would come in for Sunday dining. The restaurant sold in 2004 to Forrest Miller.

The Favazzas, a well-known restaurant family, also has a history in Little Italy. Vito, Sr. operated Flee's at 1025 Franklin from 1952-1958. The new Favazza's, interestingly enough, is located at 5201 Southwest, the exact reverse of the earlier restaurant's street address and was established on the Hill by Vito, Sr., his wife, Ellen, and Anthony, Vito, Jr.

Among the other more elegant dining places were two dating back before the 1920s. These were Joe Garavelli's at DeBaliviere

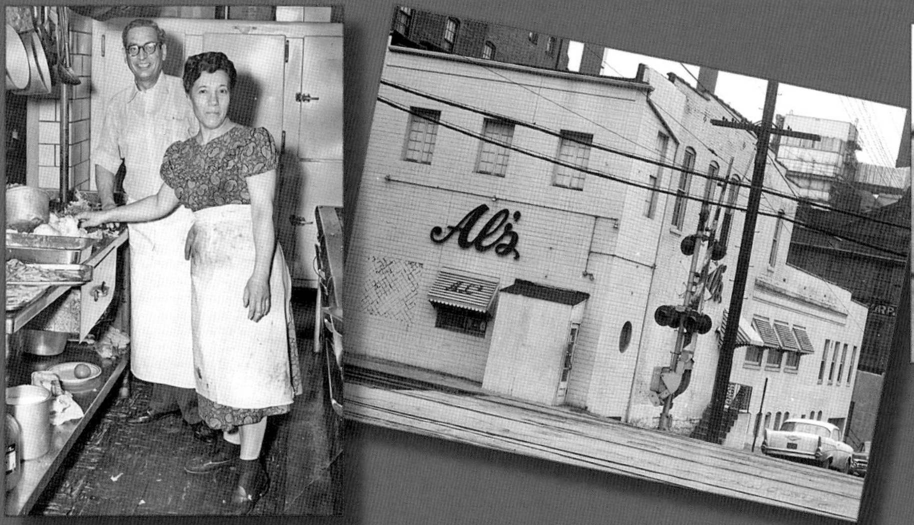

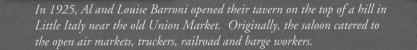

*In 1925, Al and Louise Barroni opened their tavern on the top of a hill in Little Italy near the old Union Market. Originally, the saloon catered to the open air markets, truckers, railroad and barge workers.*

*Many great meals with good friends have been enjoyed in the restaurants pictured above.*

71

and De Giverville, and Cafferata's at Delmar and Taylor.

For a special-occasion destination, Garavelli's was the choice destination. With its proximity to Washington University, it catered to students and professors alike and the ambience was inspiring. You might find Joe, the owner, carving the beef or ham in the cafeteria in the front part of the building or overseeing the dining room in the back. Joe, was universally liked and admired. Joseph Garavelli was born in Bassignana, Alessandria, in 1884, and came to America in 1909. Soon after his arrival he started in the restaurant business with his brother, Peter, then owner of the Garavelli Buffet at Grand and Olive Street. Later he was employed at Cafferata's which was located on Delmar Boulevard. In 1913, he opened his bar and, as the 1940 newspapers quoted, "Garavelli's has expanded and grown into one of the most beautiful restaurants in St. Louis, a National Institution. The restaurant serves an average of 3,000 people a day. It is, indeed, so beautiful that two pages have been devoted to it in *Missouri's Contribution to American Architecture* by J.A. Bryan. In the center of the dining room, a marble fountain made by Mr. A.P. Nardini of Boston, can be admired. In the rear, a large cage, taking two-thirds of the wall, has been built in, and provided with small trees and little fountains. There one finds all sorts of exotic birds: canaries from all corners of the earth, all contributing to make Garavelli's

*Agostino's, a family-operated Italian restaurant since 1967, owned the prominent landmark, pictured above, a hundred-year-old building, which was completely renovated by Agostino and Rosa Gabriele at the corner of Manchester and Clarkson. The family is a proud recipient of the DiRona, Mobile Dining, and Five Star Diamond awards. At left, Agostino Gabriele is photographed for the cover of a national magazine.*

an artistic and beautiful place. All around one finds tapestries and various other objects of art. Mr. Garavelli, through his popularity, has indeed done more than any other man to keep high the name of the Italians in the city. If Joe were to run for mayor he would be elected. It is not necessary to add here that Garavelli's cuisine and service are unsurpassable."

Cicardi's, like Garavelli's, was also an elegant special-occasion destination during the teens and the twenties. Its building and interior was featured in national architectural magazines. This five-star restaurant on the corner of Euclid and Delmar in the West End was a favored meeting place for the Italian members of the Fratellanza, a national, mutual-aid society active in St. Louis since 1866.

Restaurants have evolved a great deal since Midge Berra sat solving the world's problems at the Brass Key. Today, there are over 500 restaurant choices in St. Louis, many of them independently owned, especially those offering Italian cuisine. But it was here in St. Louis where it started - great Italian restaurants serving up food so good, it makes it impossible to dare take a chance on Italian food in any other North American city.

*Andreino DeSantis (shown with some famous customers), newly arrived from Italy, was an innovator who initiated "fine dining." Dominic and Jackie Galati, in 1971, purchased Andreino's which became Dominic's. Andreino is pictured at right with Frank Sinatra and Dean Martin; below, from left to right, with Michael Landon and Milton Berle.*

*Lou and Nancy Boccardi, opened Lou Boccardi's in 1972 on the edge of the Hill near Urzi's Italian Market. Lou Boccardi's was famous both for its St. Louis-style pizza and other Italian offerings and is currently run by their daughter, Lilly.*

*At Edwards and Bischoff, Lou "Spotty" Oldani opened Oldani's in 1932. Located near Ruggeri's, Oldani's did an excellent job at handling the overflow from that legendary restaurant. In 1960, Oldani's was sold. The location later became Mama Campisi's.*

73

# RUGGERI'S

Mama "Minnie" Ruggeri is pictured with her son-in-law, Frank. Erminia, "Minnie," with her husband, Henry, the "Chief" Ruggeri, Sr., opened the legendary Ruggeri's in 1934. She loved nothing better than to make sure that all her waiters were properly married to "nice Italian girls."

*"As little boys on the Hill, we sat playing under the streetlight and, almost every night, a car would pull up and someone would poke their head out of the window and ask us, "How do we get to Ruggeri's?"*

It has been said that Ruggeri's Restaurant exuded a unique charm that set it apart from every restaurant in the world! One might ask "What then sets Ruggeri's apart?" Their food or famous recipes could not be the sole answer to their great popularity. It can only be the Ruggeri family! Theirs is a history not simply of a business but of a wonderful family who made everyone who walked through their door feel the warmth of their welcome.

More than a half a century ago in March 1934 Henry Ruggeri, Sr. and his wife, Erminia, who was affectionately called "Minnie," originally opened a restaurant on the corner of Edwards Street and Elizabeth Avenue. The location first served as a corner tavern operated by Antonio Ruggeri, Henry, Sr.'s father. After Antonio's death in 1927 the tavern was occupied by several businessmen until 1934. It was then that George Pirone, Sr., the current tavern owner, vacated the site and Henry, Sr. and Minnie started their business. Minnie was the cook and Henry was both waiter and bartender. Their first employee was Frank Ruggeri who would later marry their daughter, Josephine. A son, Henry, Jr. joined the business in the early 1950s.

The restaurant gradually gained a reputation of serving great "charcoal broiled steaks" and a wide choice of seafood dishes in addition to Italian favorites. The restaurant pioneered a multi-paged menu offering its patrons wide choices in beef, seafood, veal, chicken, and pasta dishes. This type of menu was a first since it was only seen in hotel dining rooms. However, longtime waiter, Mickey Garagiola, who was with Ruggeri's since day one, remembers that for many years there was no menu. He approached patrons and said, "What do you want? Steak, chicken, fish, or spaghetti? And, of course, after a whiff of the sizzling beef and garlic, most said steak."

Several expansions over the years culminated in 1956 with a larger kitchen, banquet room, and a la carte dining room with a seating capacity of 450 persons. Entertainment was provided nightly by Stan Kann who played a Wurlitzer theatre pipe organ.

Ruggeri's Restaurant from the very early days seemed to be a magnet for local and national politicians. It was also common to be dining next to such national celebrities as the Cisco Kid and his sidekick Pancho, Jack Dempsey, Primo Carnera, Max Baer, Robert Taylor, Vince Lombardi, Mickey Mantle, and Joe DiMaggio. One story has it that Frank Sinatra at midnight knocked on Ruggeri's back door after hours trying to get a late dinner for him and his band. He was denied special admittance because he had not yet hit the big time nor could, in his early years, court special treatment.

One New Year's Eve, Hack, employed at the Chase Park Plaza, called saying Mae West was coming in with a party of ten after her

Russo's Cucina.

Mama worked alongside her three sons: Luigi helped in the kitchen, Tony waited tables, and Frank tended bar. Formerly, Luigi learned and worked under the tutelage of Joe and Lou Parente.

Frozen pizzas became the rage of St. Louis during the 1950s and 1960s. The Meglios owned a frozen pizza plant at 611 Tower Grove and many grocery stores carried Luigi's frozen pizza and they were distributed in 39 states. In 1959, Luigi's established a second location at 8965 Natural Bridge at Springdale, Bel Ridge. Then a third opened its doors on Manchester Road in 1966 in the former El Avion restaurant. The grand opening for restaurant number four was in the early 1970s at Village Square in Hazelwood.

A new generation stepped up to take the reins of the empire as Tony's son, John opened Meglio's Italian Grill and Bar at 12490 St. Charles Rock Road and announced,

"We sold 16,000 pizzas in each of our first two years in business. Our homemade sausage and family secret recipes have proved delicious for 55 years."

Also purveyors of the growing pizza trend in the early 1950s were Sam "Chiefy" Antinora, and his brother, Mike, owners of the Isle of Capri on Macklind. Recognized as one of the five pioneer pizza places in St. Louis, it was later bought out by Charlie Gitto, Sr. The Isle of Capri Pizza served Neapolitan thin-crust pizza, sliced like a pie. Also popular remembers Charlie Gitto, Sr. was the "spenguni" thick-crust, square Sicilian-style pizza.

Many old-time pizza lovers will recall number four in the St Louis pizza hall of fame–Paul Cusanelli on West Pine (No surprise that Paul Cusanelli's father came from Pietraoia, near Naples, the home and birthplace of Antonio Meglio, Sr., of Luigi's Pizza fame, and for that matter of pizza itself in the 1700s.

While pizza in the Midwest began with Amedeo Fio-

*The Imo family, left to right, Mary, Frank, Carol, Ed, Vince, Marge, John, and Carl.*

*The original Imo's opened at 1907 Thurman in 1964.*

*Sam "Chiefy" Antinora, in the orange shirt at left, and his brother, Mike, owned the Isle of Capri, one of the five early pizza places in St. Louis. Mike Antinora, Jr., currently works as manager of Favazza's restaurant on the Hill. The Isle of Capri was sold in the mid-1950s to Charlie Gitto, Sr., who currently owns Charlie Gitto's Downtown in St. Louis.*

79

re of Melrose Pizzeria, it is only fitting that the story of the first five pizza places in St. Louis end with Amedeo or at least his location. As mentioned, Melrose became Parente's. In 1954, Parentes sold to Rossino's. a name created from the partnership Roy and Lee Russo (brother of Annie Gitto, wife of Charlie, Sr.) and Frank Gianino. The latter left the picture, leaving Nancy Russo (sister to Mary Rose Del Pietro) and Tom Zimmerman to help run the place, buying it from Nancy's parents in 1963. Sadly, Rossino's closed its doors in February 2006 ending a great era of St. Louis pizza tradition.

One of the early spin-off success stories focuses on Marge and Eddie Imo who built their empire by franchising their St. Louis-style pizza. Imo's was born at 1907 Thurman in November, 1964. During that time, Marge and Eddie rented a home at 5211 Wilson. Marge fondly recalls enjoying Parente's thin-crust pizza with Provel cheese, as well as Gitto's Isle of Capri on Macklind. Although people identify St. Louis-style pizza with Imo's, Marge is quick to correct that they only popularized it and brought it to the masses.

Off I-64 near Hampton, many will remember and recognize the Imo's neon pizza chef–a beacon for the "Provel-deficient."

However, in 1964, they were the first to offer delivery and take-out service. In the 1970s they purchased Costa grocery downtown on Franklin after Tony Costa died. Costa's sold the Provel cheese used to make the ever more popular St. Louis-style pizza. Moving Costa's to 2600 Big Bend, Imo's renamed it Roma's.

As to the distribution of Provel cheese, the family partnered with Abel 'Toots' Pezzani. Currently Imo's has 94 restaurants (80 in Greater St. Louis) and 14 throughout Missouri, Illinois, and Kansas. Imo's ships their pizza to 48 states daily.

"Ed and I are proud of the wonderful success stories about how delivery personnel have actually ended up owning franchises," Marge remarks and also announces, "Our 50th anniversary is around the corner. We hope to celebrate by opening up the 100th franchise."

It all started in St. Louis with Amedeo Fiori, then the hand off to Parentes, Isle of Capri, Luigi's, Cusanelli's and Rossino's. Now pick up the phone book and count the number of pizza places in St. Louis (450) and remember those who went before and got the dough rolling.

Joe Parente, at left, is cousin to Bart Saracino, patriarch of the Bartolino's restaurants. Both were cousins from their home base in San Martino. Joe Parente, old-timers will remember, in 1947 purchased Melrose Pizza, the first pizza restaurant in the Midwest, and through his and his brother, Lou's efforts, popularized pizza in the St. Louis area.

Lou Parente with his mother, Concetta Parente, in San Marco Piazza in Venice in 1953. Joe and his brother, Lou, invented St. Louis thin crust pizza, using Provel cheese. This pizza was popularized to the masses by Imo's.

Joe Boccardi, in the restaurant business from the early '70s, pictured at left, stands next to Joe Parente. The Parentes sponsored both the Boccardis and the Saracinos [Bartolino's Restaurant] to come to America. Between the three families, 20 restaurants in St. Louis area have spun off.

*Restaurant owners from several St. Louis Italian dining establishments (circa 1950) pose with Italian boxer, Anthony Parrino. Left to right:*
*Roy Russo, Vince Bommarito, Bob Casullo, Charlie Gitto, Parrino, Julius "Biggie" Garagnani, Lou Parente, and Gene Shiavo.*

With both its classy AND "mom 'n pop" Italian restaurants, the St. Louisan enjoys impeccable, elegant, romantic, and innovative Italian-American cuisine. St. Louis has it all with its great number of authentic, Italian eateries, many of them, now served by a third and fourth generation. In our first book *The Hill: Its History, Its Recipes* we featured Charlie Gitto's "On The Hill," Dominic's, Cunetto's, and Giovanni's.

Expanding from but still including the Hill repertoire we move out to other endearing and welcoming enclaves; Yacovelli's and Lombardo's in the north to Portabella's and Café Napoli in Clayton and never to forget the crowning glory of Tony's and Kemoll's downtown St. Louis. This list of 20 restaurants is not complete but for nostalgia, checkered and white tablecloths, homemade, traditional, and traditional with a twist, you will not go wrong. St. Louis foodies are in for a treat and will relish the real Italian food experience contained in the following pages.

81

# Bartolino's

*Pictured is the Bartolino family of restaurateurs, left to right: Bart, Jr., John, Bart, Sr., Michael, and Chris.*

The crown jewel of the Saracino family restaurant tradition is Bartolino's. Bart Saracino, Sr. founded his Italian eatery on Hampton Avenue in South St. Louis in 1969. Since then, it has become a classic St. Louis place with an extremely devoted following. For his remarkable contribution to the restaurant community, the St. Louis Restaurant Association awarded him the prestigious title of Restaurateur of the Year in 2002. Not bad for a man who came from a very humble beginning.

Born to a family of eight children in the Italian province of Abruzzi not far from Rome, Bart, Sr. immigrated to St. Louis in 1954. Sponsored by cousins, Joe and Lou Parente, the young man started American life working in Parente's Italian Village at Chippewa and Lansdowne. He not only learned the ropes of the restaurant business but fell in love with the coat-check girl, Roseanne Lafata. The child of Palermo immigrants, Nick and Rose Lafata, the young woman proudly accepted Bart's hand in marriage.

Together with Roseanne's parents, the young couple opened LaCino's Pizza in 1961. While raising four young children, the opportunity arrived they couldn't pass up. In 1969,

Cousin Joe Parente's Mama Parente's Restaurant came up for sale, so Bart and Roseanne siezed the moment and the rest is history.

The restaurant business has evolved into a family affair. As Bart, Jr. likes to say, "There is no 'I in Team.' We all benefit from our family members' assistance." Under this principle, Bartolino's South on South Lindbergh was founded in 1983 and, soon after, Chris' Pancake and Dining on Southwest Avenue was established in 1987.

As for Bart's namesake, Bart Jr., it is a reminder that he is carrrying on a family tradition, a concept instilled in him and his brothers, John, Michael, and Chris.

In 2008, Bartolino's moved from its long-time home on Hampton to the newly constructed Drury Inn at the corner of Wilson and Hampton. Christening the new establishment as Bartolino's Osteria, guests will often be greeted by Bart, Jr. and Michael.

Besides a Mediterranean décor that makes you feel you are dining somewhere in sun-drenched Italy, Bartolino's Osteria boasts a native Sicilian executive chef. According to Bart, Jr., Gianfranco Munna offers up a "…gourmet and continental blend of Italian dishes from an ambitious menu featuring cuisine from different regions of Italy, north and south. Not only that, the list of wines has been specifically selected to complement the menu offerings."

Every family member helps each other with their three restaurants. However, the Saracino generosity goes beyond the family circle. The Saracinos contribute faithfully to the American Cancer Society's Taste of Italy as well as to Dining Out for Life, a multi-restaurant effort to support AIDS research. And for the past 40 years the family has laid out a delectable spread at Hampton-Midtown Kiwanis Club's Annual Ravioli Dinner. This is a special event held for underprivileged children. Since no good deeds go unrewarded, the City of Missouri and Governor Bob Holden appointed Bart, Jr. to the St. Louis Police Board in 2002.

Though only in Missouri for little more than half a century, the Saracino family has certainly made an impressive impact on the Gateway City. Not content, in the last 40 years to found restaurants beloved by city and county dweller alike, they have given back to the community. Now with a new generation of 13 grandchildren, there is also no doubt the Saracino family will continue to contribute to the St. Louis landscape by founding yet more delicious eateries. There is also no doubt that their generosity to St. Louis will also continue as they perform more acts of public service and generously contribute to local charities. As outstanding, St. Louisans, there is no doubt that more jewels will be added to the family crown.

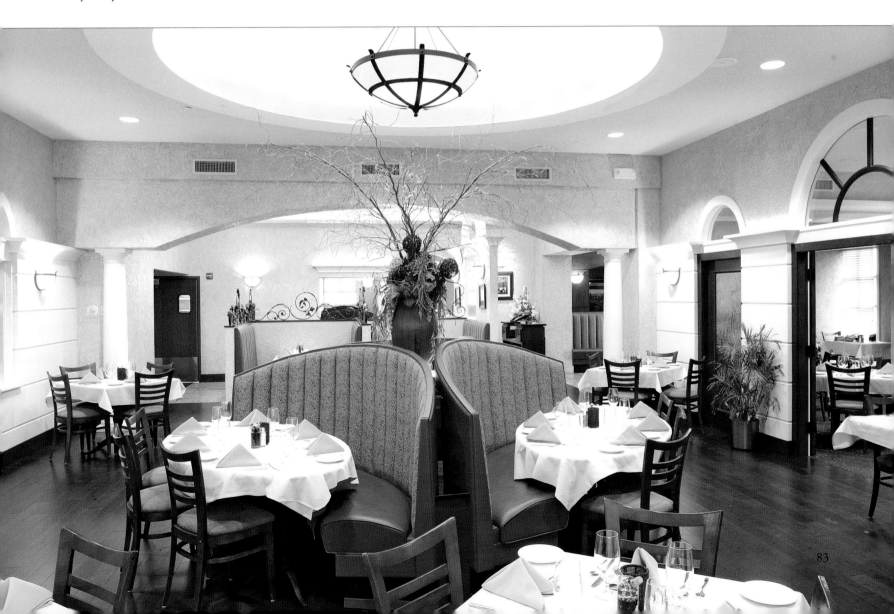

*Bart, Sr. and Roseanne on Devonshire in the mid-1960s with, left to right, Mike, Bart, Jr., and John.*

*Above: Bart, Sr. picks grapes at his ancestral home in Italy with his sister-in-law, Michalina. And, photo left, Bart, Sr. is producing "the nectar of the gods." at his family's farm.*

84

# AUSTRALIAN BARRAMUNDI IN CRAZY WATER

INGREDIENTS

2½ lbs. barramundi filet with skin,
    cut in 8-oz. fillets

Salt and pepper to taste

1 tsp. seafood seasoning blend

3 tbsp. extra-virgin olive oil

1 tsp. crushed red pepper flakes

3 cloves garlic, crushed

¼ cup green queen olives
    (large, green, mild)

3 tbsp. white onions, cut julienne

6 whole artichoke hearts

6 fingerling potatoes

6 pieces fresh fennel

½ cup white wine

¼ cup Pernod (anise-flavored
    liqueur)

1 qt. lobster stock

Chopped fresh parsley

Crusty bread for serving

Season fish with salt, pepper, and seafood seasoning. Cook skin-side down as desired until skin is crisp.

Heat large sauté skillet over medium heat. Cook extra-virgin olive oil, red pepper, garlic, olives, onion, artichokes, potatoes, and fennel until tender. Deglaze by adding wine and Pernod, stirring pieces from bottom of pan. Add lobster stock. Heat until broth comes to simmer. Cook 3 to 5 minutes to combine flavors.

Serve fish in shallow bowls with plenty of crazy broth. Garnish with parsley and fennel. Have plenty of crusty bread on hand for dipping, dunking, and mopping.

SERVES 4

*Bartolino's Chef Gianfranco Munna from Sicily.*

That same approach won him his bride, Kathy, a lovely flight attendant he met in 1980. Set up as a blind date by a friend, Tony charmed the young lady at the top of the Westport Gold Tower. "We danced one dance, then never left the floor."

There is no more splendid a place to "see and be seen" than in Café Napoli. Seated on the outdoor patio on a glorious, sun-drenched afternoon, enjoying the succulent flavors of a Florentine appetizer like crostini followed by a mouth-watering Neapolitan specialty such as linguine marechiano or linguine ischia, cannot be topped. Well, maybe a warm hand on your shoulder when Tony passes by. After, you can repair to Bar Napoli for a cocktail. Featuring a wine cellar room, you can hold a private party and continue to enjoy the delectable food, ambience and Tony's fateful charm until the wee hours of the morning.

Recently, his once-orphaned sister visited from Italy. Standing outside Café Napoli, she embraced him and tearfully proclaimed, " I am so proud!"

Tony has not prospered alone. As in soccer, you are part of a team. In this case, his team is his loving family. He encouraged his brother, Nick, to move to Cincinnati and open, Nicola's and Via Vite. Nick's son, Christian, is following in his illustrious uncle's footsteps and is fast becoming one of the premier chefs of America. While establishing son, Ande, in a brand-new restaurant enterprise, Napoli 2ue at Woodsmill and Clayton, he is readying to hand over Café Napoli into the capable hands of his equally charming son, Kye.

Despite not becoming a soccer great, Tony's detours led to some pretty wonderful adventures. If it weren't for a damaged cartilage in his knee, St. Louis would never have had the opportunity of being home to a charming man and a restaurant institution that will hopefully remain with us for a long, long time to come. So yes, sport came first, then the food. But, wait. Once Kye takes the reins of Café Napoli, Tony will probably return to sport. Not soccer, but golf. Maybe he can get one of his golf idols from the restaurant photos to improve his score. "I shoot in the 90s, but I'm still striving for the 80s," confesses the athletic owner. Let's hope your next detour will get you a hole-in-one.

# RIGATONI SORRENTINA

INGREDIENTS

*Extra-virgin olive oil*

*8 oz. arugula*

*1 tsp. oregano*

*2 tbsp. chopped garlic*

*Salt and black pepper*

*1 tsp. red pepper*

*3 cups basic tomato sauce*

*1 lb. rigatoni*

*1/3 lb. Mozzarella di Bufala,*

*cut in cubes*

*¼ cup fresh basil leaves*

In a 12-inch sauce pan, heat olive oil until smoking. Cook arugula, oregano, garlic, salt and peppers, stirring often, until arugula is wilted and garlic is lightly browned. Add tomato sauce. Simmer until reduced as desired.

Meanwhile, bring large pot of salted water to a boil. Cook pasta until al dente. Drain. Add to sauce. Toss in Mozzarella and fresh basil. Stir. Serve.

SERVES 6

*Tony with the legendary Kirk Douglas.*

*Being a capable golfer himself, Tony was especially pleased when Jack Nicklaus dropped by.*

*Tony poses for a photograph with his wife, Kathy, and their two sons, Ande and Kye (in front).*

*Ande welcomes a future Baseball Hall-of-Famer, Albert Pujols, who takes time off to have a great meal at Cafe Napoli.*

*County and Western singer/songwriter Trace Adkins stands outside the restaurant with Tony and Ande.*

*Two popular St. Louis figures, Jack Buck and the former basketball coach for Saint Louis University, Charlie Spoonhauer, enjoy a laugh with Tony.*

# VEAL CHOP VINO ROSSO

### INGREDIENTS

*16 oz. veal Porterhouse*

*1 tbsp. salt*

*1 tbsp. freshly cracked black pepper*

*¼ cup extra-virgin olive oil*

*2 tbsp. garlic, minced*

*1 lb. assorted mushrooms (shiitake, porcini, fresh white button, portobello), sliced*

*1 tsp. red pepper*

*¼ cup Worcestershire sauce*

*½ cup dry red wine*

*2 cups beef stock*

*2 tbsp. unsalted butter*

Preheat grill. Season veal chop with a bit of salt and pepper. Rub with a little garlic and olive oil. Set aside.

Heat ¼ cup olive oil in a Dutch oven. Before oil starts to smoke, add garlic and mushrooms. Season with salt, black, and red pepper. Cook, stirring often, until cooked thoroughly. Add Worcestershire sauce, red wine, and beef stock. Cook until reduced by half. Stir butter into reduced sauce, mixing until melted and well incorporated in wine sauce.

Meanwhile, grill veal chops 7 to 9 minutes per side for medium-rare or to desired temperature. Serve butter sauce over veal.

SERVES 3

# Charlie Gitto's Downtown

*The patriarch of a family of restaurateurs, Charlie Gitto, Sr. appears with his daughter, Karen Vangel.*

Thirty years ago on November 18, 1974, in an unassuming brick building, in the shadows of the skyscrapers of downtown St. Louis, a little colonial outpost of the Hill sprung to life on Sixth Street. Since that time it has become a magnet for American Presidents, movie stars, sports heroes, baseball fans, tourists, and everyday St. Louisans. This little building is the home of Charlie Gitto's Downtown, founded by Charlie Gitto, Sr. in 1974.

It is unlikely that Charlie Gitto's father, George, ever imagined that he would be the patriarch of a great American culinary family. Born in Messina, Sicily in 1903, George Gitto would immigrate with his family, first to Boston's Little Italy, then to St. Louis. In America, George married Francesca, still the proud matriarch of the Gitto clan at 101.

Young Charlie Gitto did not grow up with dreams of elegant dining rooms and plates of delicious pasta. Instead, the child Charlie had a cobbler's vision of soft Italian leather and finely hewn soles. Charlie remembers, "My Dad worked making shoes at the Peacock store, and I used to go around the house saying, 'When I grow up, I am going to make shoes.'" But childhood expectations would give way to a whole other life when the adolescent Charlie took his first job in a restaurant.

Charlie Gitto, Sr. started his career as a busboy in the great Hill restaurant, Ruggeri's. He soon moved up to the position of maitre 'd at Stan Musial and Biggie's. It was there that Charlie first discovered his gifts as a restaurateur. "I loved dressing up in a tuxedo, loved greeting the customers. Tell me your name once and I never forgot it."

During this time of vocational discovery, Charlie also found his soul-mate, Annie, his wife of 60 years. It seems that Charlie's and Annie's romantic fate had been set from the very beginning of their lives: as Charlie grew up at 5400 Bischoff on the Hill, while Annie was raised at 5300 Bischoff. Yet, despite their very close proximity, it took a considerable amount of time for either of them to know that the other one existed. In fact, they never even met until after their respective grade school graduations. It took so long because, as Charlie muses, "I went to Catholic school and she went to public school and we never messed with the public school girls."

With Annie's support, Charlie broke ground on the Gitto family restaurant tradition in the 1950s when he operated one of St. Louis' first pizza parlors, the Isle of Capri. As was the case with many Italian eateries, Charlie's pizza place was a family operation. His wife, Annie, who had learned food preparation from her mother, Nuncia Russo, cooked and supported her husband every step of the way. "She is a fantastic helpmate and cook, "Charlie says proudly of Annie. "She helped the kids get started in their own restaurants. I would stick by her through anything life throws at us."

The same loyalty can be found in Annie, as she was the one who encouraged Charlie to take the next big step, to raise money to buy a building in downtown St. Louis, and then to open his own Italian restaurant under his own name.

At the age of 45, Charlie Gitto, Sr. bought the business, and transformed the former Pasta House into the Charlie Gitto's Restaurant of today. Charlie has done quite well with his venture on Sixth Street.

Today, a sign outside the restaurant's window states, "Charlie Gitto welcomes baseball fans," a simple reminder of how popular this St.

Louis institution has become with sports fans. Upon entering it becomes immediately apparent that the popularity of this restaurant goes well beyond Cardinals' and Cubs' fans coming for a bite after a summer ballgame, as the walls are covered with the photographs of American Presidents Reagan and Clinton; sports legends like Joe DiMaggio, Joe Garagiola, and Jimmy Connors; literary giants like Tennessee Williams; and American institutions like Bob Hope, Harry Caray, Howard Cosell, and good friend Tommy Lasorda; all visitors to Charlie Gitto's establishment on Sixth Street.

About a decade ago Famous Barr offered to buy the building from Charlie but he turned them down, saying, "What was I going to do with the rest of my life?" Certainly, all kinds of popular hobbies of the retired come to mind, but the man who never forgets a name does not belong on a golf course or in a fishing boat. He belongs in the restaurant, the St. Louis institution he created, where Charlie makes sure every patron is made to feel welcome and satisfied, whether it be Channel 5 or the St. Louis Cardinals ordering trays of food; baseball fans relaxing over burgers and beer; or conventioneers partaking of the delicious entrees and enjoying the wealth of riches on the restaurant's impressive wine list.

From the strong foundation built by Charlie and Annie, a new generation of Gitto restaurateurs has arisen. Their daughter, Karen, alongside her father, and her husband, Jim Vangel, work at Charlie Gitto's Downtown. The Vangel children, Louie and Francesca, have recently begun helping out during college breaks. Another of Charlie Sr.'s sons, Charlie, Jr., has made a marvelous success of Charlie Gitto's "On the Hill" and at Harrah's Casino in Maryland Heights. Another son, Johnny, provides premier casual dining, live entertainment, and a late-night karaoke club at Johnny Gitto's on Chippewa in South City.

The family still has fond memories of Charlie's third son, George.

In a time when the constant march of franchises threaten to make the City of St. Louis into just another piece of Generica, Charlie Gitto, Sr. and his family show that originality will always reign supreme.

# Pasta Messina

*A longtime popular menu entrée, Pasta Messina was named in honor of Charlie's father, George, who was born in Messina, Sicily in 1903.*

INGREDIENTS

1 lb. linguini noodles

1 red onion, sliced

1 red bell pepper, sliced

1 cup chicken breast, diced

1 lb. shrimp, peeled, deveined

1 cup portobello mushrooms, sliced

1 cup chicken stock

1 cup tomato sauce

1 tbsp. garlic, fresh chopped

½ tsp. salt

½ tsp. red pepper

¼ cup olive oil

Sauté the red onion, red bell pepper, diced chicken, shrimp, and mushrooms in olive oil along with salt, red pepper, and garlic. Deglaze with chicken stock. Add tomato sauce. Simmer for 2-3 minutes. Serve over pasta.

SERVES 4

*Charlie celebrates a birthday with his charming daughter, Karen, and his lovely wife, Annie.*

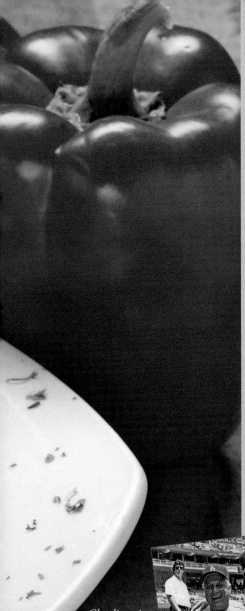

*Charlie enjoys baseball as much as Tommy Lasorda and Whitey Herzog.*

*Another baseball legend with Italian heritage, Joe Torre, joins Charlie at the restaurant.*

Charlie Gitto's
Downtown

*John and Jimmy Connors join Charlie for a good-natured photograph.*

*"Paulie" in the* Rocky *film series, Burt Young, and Charlie have become close over the years.*

*A handsome couple: Charlie and Annie Gitto.*

# STEAK FRANCESCA

*Steak Francesca was added to the menu in appreciation of Charlie Gitto's granddaughter, Francesca, daughter of Karen Gitto-Vangel in appreciation for her taking breaks from her college studies to help out in the family enterprise.*

### INGREDIENTS

| | |
|---|---|
| 14 oz. sirloin strip steak | ½ cup white wine |
| 2 cups chicken stock | 1 cup shiitake mushrooms |
| ¼ cup lemon juice | ½ cup Prosciutto ham, diced |
| ¼ cup butter, melted | ½ cup seasoned breadcrumbs |
| ½ cup flour | 1 cup Provolone cheese, shredded |

Grill steak to preferred doneness. In medium pot, add chicken stock, lemon juice, and white wine and bring to a boil. In a separate bowl, whip butter and flour until thick. Add this to the pot and cook until the sauce thickens. Add shredded Provolone cheese, mushrooms, and ham. Roll steak in breadcrumbs then top with cheese. Pour warm sauce over steak.

SERVES 2

*Three generations of a culinary family, left to right, Lee Russo, her grandson Marc, co-owner of Luciano's in Clayton, and his mother, Mary Rose Del Pietro.*

## Del Pietro's

The story of Del Pietro's House of Pasta is certainly a tale of hard work, dedication, and family loyalty, but above all else, it is the illustrative history of the power and strength of the Italian woman.

The story begins not in St. Louis, but in Bicoquine, Sicily, the birthplace of Mary Faille Palazzola, matriarch of what would become a St. Louis restaurant empire. In 1904, Mary crossed the ocean to America and settled in Rome, Georgia. Though her English was poor and the setting of the American South entirely unfamiliar, there in Rome she opened a small, but successful diner. For the next twenty years, Mary tirelessly ran her little establishment while simultaneously raising her children.

But by 1926, Mary had grown weary of the decidedly non-Italian setting of Rome, Georgia. Desiring to be closer to family and to live in a community with a strong Italian population, Mary and her children moved again, this time to St. Louis.

Mary's children observed their mother's courage and dedication, and they absorbed the lessons of her impressive example. From the bedrock foundation Mary had laid, her daughter, Lee, and Lee's husband, Rosario (Roy) Russo, took over in 1954 one of St. Louis' earliest pizza places, located near St. Louis University at the corner of Sarah and West Pine, Rossino's. Lee Russo still remembers the pizza she and her husband served to so many college students, saying, "It was a thin crust pizza, and pineapple and peaches besides anchovies and shrimp were popular toppings."

Thus, Roy and Lee's daughter, Mary Rose, was born into a family where both her mother and her grandmother were successful restaurateurs. From an early age, Mary Rose knew that she would follow their example. Indeed, by age 11, she was working at Rossino's. She met Michael Del Pietro at St. Ambrose Parochial School. Growing up, they lived on the same block. Michael's parents owned the Brown Derby, a tavern by old Sportman's Park. In 1965, Mary Rose and Michael married, and soon after, they teamed up with her parents, Roy and Lee, to open Saro's, a restaurant in the old Parente's location at the corner of Lansdowne and Chippewa. For the next 15 years the family made a success of Saro's, even mentoring Pasta House Company founders Kim Tucci and John Ferraro, both who were employed by Rossino's in their early years.

But in 1976, in conjunction with the American Bicentennial, Mary Rose made her own declaration of independence by stepping out on her own with husband Michael and forming Del Pietro's House of Pasta at 5625 Hampton Avenue in St. Louis Hills.

"We chose this location," Mary Rose remembers, " the old Vincenzo's and also home to the first KFC in St. Louis, because we lived just down the street on Tamm Avenue. Initially, I cooked and Michael worked the front, and we both wore all the hats. We could not afford laundry service, so every night I packed up the table linens to wash and iron at home. Also, since we could not afford a babysitter, the children, from kindergarten on, came to the restaurant after school to set tables and fold napkins. They fell asleep in the kitchen with pans banging, and we tucked them in with a tablecloth."

Eventually, Mary Rose's and Michael's hard work and sacrifice paid off, and the business became a profitable concern, thereby allowing the couple to not only expand the capacity of the restaurant considerably from its original eight tables to its present state which includes a bar, banquet rooms, and seating for 200. In addition, they established a whole new restaurant, Michael's, at 141 and Olive.

Tragically, Michael passed away in 1985, leaving Mary Rose to raise four children and run two restaurants. With so much responsibility placed upon her shoulders, Mary Rose had no choice but to sell Michael's and to focus her attention on Del Pietro's.

Having been born into this amazing restaurant family and raised in the warm familiarity of their parents' restaurant kitchen, it is not surprising that Mary Rose's and Michael's four children have all become impressive restaurant owners in their own right.

Sons Michael and Marc both attended the prestigious Culinary Institute of America. Marc worked at Le Cirque in Paris and Hotel de Paris in Monaco, while Michael has served as chef for Luciano's. In 2002, Marc, Michael and sister, Lea, co-founded Luciano's in Clayton, which is located adjacent to the Ritz Carlton. In addition, son Michael also operates the popular Kilkenny's Irish Pub in Clayton. Finally, daughter Angela and her husband, Thomas Zoog, own and operate the

elegant and fashionable restaurant, Portabella's, also located in Clayton.

Looking back over the 32-year history of Del Pietro's, Mary Rose is proud of how the restaurant has stayed true to the Sicilian dishes, greatly enjoyed by her faithful clientele. When she is asked about retirement, she shakes her head saying, "I love my customers. I am loyal to my longtime staff. There is nothing else I would rather be doing."

Mary Rose Del Pietro has worked hard, taken chances and suffered setbacks, but she has always overcome the obstacles placed before her and she has set a wonderful example for her children. She is a woman of her line, and her grandmother, Mary Faille Palazzola, would be proud.

# PARMESAN-ENCRUSTED PORK CHOPS

### INGREDIENTS

3 or 4 pork rib chops     Coarse salt and white pepper

1 cup seasoned breadcrumbs     ¼ cup olive oil

½ cup Parmigiano Reggiano cheese     2 tbsp. unsalted butter

Preheat oven to 450 degrees.

Mix breadcrumbs and cheese. Season pork chops with salt and white pepper, then coat with breadcrumb mixture.

In oven-safe pan, heat olive oil and butter until butter starts to brown. Add chops. Bake in preheated oven 6 to 8 minutes. Flip them over. Continue to cook 6 to 8 minutes longer. Let rest 3 to 5 minutes before serving.

Serve hot pork chops with sausage and gnocchi (see below) ladled on top. Garnish with fresh parsley and other desired herbs.

SERVES 4

## SAUSAGE AND GNOCCHI

### INGREDIENTS

2 tbsp. butter, divided

3 cups gnocchi (preparation below)

2 bell peppers, roasted

2 cups cooked Italian sausage

½ cup chopped Italian parsley

12 oz. pork or chicken broth

Heat 1 tablespoon butter over medium heat until it starts to brown. Cook gnocchi (see below) in butter until it begins to brown. Add roasted pepper and cooked sausage. Taste and adjust seasoning as necessary. Add parsley and broth. When liquid boils and starts to coat the mixture, add remaining 1 tablespoon butter. Heat just until it melts. Serve immediately over pork chops.

### PARMIGIANO GNOCCHI

Mix together 1 pound Ricotta cheese, ½ cup grated Parmigiano cheese, 2 teaspoons salt and 1 egg until smooth. Mix in about 1 cup flour, adding more until mixture just comes together in soft dough. Roll in ½-inch ropes and cut in 1-inch lengths. Cook in boiling salted water about 8 minutes until they start to float. Using slotted spoon, remove from water.

*Rosario and Lee Russo with daughter, Mary Rose, Easter Sunday in the late 1940s.*

*Lee Russo with daughters, Nancy, at left, and Mary Rose at 5319 Bischoff.*

*Mary Rose's offspring: Semicircling from bottom left are Olivia Zoog, Angela Del Pietro Zoog, Lea, Marc, and Michael Del Pietro, and Mary Rose holding Isabella Zoog.*

*Mary Rose and Michael Del Pietro, Sr. circa 1965.*

# SFINCI

## A SICILIAN DESSERT

Mary Rose Del Pietro: "*My mother taught me to make this Sicilian dessert and my children and grandchildren are always excited when they see these light golden puffs, piled high, drizzled with honey and almonds. They are delicious and simple to make. Today this type of dessert is disappearing. It's too bad because even while trying to eat a healthier diet, we are also eliminating a most basic comfort food.*"

### INGREDIENTS

*8 tbsp. (1 stick) butter, cubed*

*1 cup water*

*1/3 cup sugar*

*pinch of salt*

*1 cup flour*

*Oil for frying*

*3 eggs*

*½ cup honey, warmed*

*¼ cup almonds, slivered*

In a medium, heavy-bottomed sauce pan, bring butter, water, sugar and salt to boil. Heat, stirring with wooden spoon, until all butter is melted. Remove from heat and add the flour all at once, stirring with gusto until dough forms a ball that pulls away from the side of pan. It will be sticky. Let it cool 10 minutes, stirring occasionally to release steam.

In a heavy sauce pan, heat two inches of oil to 325 degrees using a deep fryer or a candy thermometer to measure temperature.

Using electric mixer, beat eggs, one at a time, into the dough, incorporating each well before adding the next. The dough should be loose but not runny.

To fry sfinci, dip a tablespoon first in the hot oil (to keep dough from sticking to spoon), then scoop out a spoonful of dough and drop it into the oil. Fry a few at a time, but don't overcrowd the pan. As dough begins to brown, after about 1 ½ minutes, turn them over. The sfinci will pop open and puff up to about twice their size, either slowly or at one time. Continue to fry, turning sfinci once or twice, until evenly browned. When they are done, drain them on paper towels.

At serving time, drizzle sfinci with honey and sprinkle with slivered almonds.

SERVES 6

*Gian-Tony's owner, Tony Catarinicchia.*

# Gian-Tony's

Tony Catarinicchia is something of a star. With his wonderful accent, Mediterranean countenance and exuberant manner, the co-founder and executive chef of Gian-Tony's appears to be the epitome of what a Hollywood casting agent would call the "perfect Italian chef." In fact, Tony has actually appeared in Hollywood productions such as MTV's *The Real World*. But Tony doesn't just look the part. He is the part.

Tony is a supremely gifted chef whose talents have been recognized not only by the patrons of Gian-Tony's, but also by prestigious outlets of the national culinary media. He and his delicious recipes have been featured in the pages of *Gourmet, Saveur,* and *Midwest Living* magazines, while the viewers of the Food Network were treated to him preparing his famous eggplant involtini appetizer and osso buco on *Cooking Live* with host, Sarah Moulton.

So how did this Sicilian-born talent find his way to St. Louis? Put simply, love and loyalty brought him here, while love and romance made him stay.

Born into a 1950s Sicily still struggling with the trauma inflicted on the island by the Second World War, Tony knew from an early age that families have to help one another to survive. That responsibility became manifest when Tony had to leave his home, at the young age of 17, to help support his family. He worked as a cook in Munich, Germany, learning *das deutsche Sprache*, missing the Sicilian sun and sending money home.

In 1972, Tony learned that his mother, (his family had recently immigrated to St. Louis' Hill), was dying. Wishing to pay his last respects to her, he traveled to America to be by her side to the end.

One night, Tony and his cousin decided to meet up at a local cocktail lounge. Tony saw a brown-eyed beauty with Rapunzel-length hair standing across the room. One look and he was smitten. He said to his cousin in Italian, "She will be my wife! What is the word for *danza* (dance)?" At the same time, the beauty, named Eva, eyed the good-looking man staring at her from across the room. They ended up dancing the night away, and after a short courtship, they married, thus giving St Louis an outstanding chef.

Initially, Tony worked for Aldo's Pizza in Washington, Missouri. Then on September 10, 1989, at the age of 35, he opened his own restaurant on the Hill, named Gian-Tony's, also working alongside his brother, Gian. In 1991, Tony formed a partnership with his son, Rosario, and the two have been a team ever since, commiting to keep the restaurant in the immediate family. Eva, a trained accountant, took care of the books, while Tony's Italian-speaking grandfather, Nonno Damiano, cultivated and tended the restaurant's vegetable garden.

Under the sure hands of Chef Tony, Gian-Tony's has become known throughout the St. Louis area for its excellent cuisine. Moreover, because Tony is a trained butcher, Gian-Tony's is a rarity in terms of the fresh quality of the meat it serves. As Tony says, "We sell more veal than anyone else. All cut, trimmed, and pounded here on site! Always fresh, never prepackaged." Thus, it is not surprising that Gian-Tony's osso buco is among one of its most requested items.

For the vegetarian patron, Gian-Tony's serves many dishes, with the eggplant involtini being the most popular. Tony makes this light rollup using paper-thin eggplant, spinach, and ricotta.

As for dessert, Gian-Tony's offers several selections, but the tiramisu is a favorite. Tony explains that he soaks the ladyfingers in espresso and amaretto, whips up 40% cream with egg

yolks and mascarpone cheese for the creamy layers, and spreads cocoa on the top, thereby creating a dazzling and delectable dessert.

Even after 19 years, Gian-Tony's remains a family business. Beyond Tony, Eva, and Rosario, the current general manager, Rosario's sister, Dionna, and Rosario's wife, Suzy, also run the business. Sadly, Nonno Damiano has now passed away. Suzy, the mother of two of Nonno's great-grandchildren, Elizabeth and Nico, wistfully remembers, "The hardest part was when the family lost Nonno. Tony and Eva lived in a duplex next to Nonno. He faithfully tended our restaurant garden that provided fresh eggplant, zucchini, basil, and carrots that are integral to our award-winning red sauces. You can always replace a garden, but you can never replace the gardener, and to this day, we all miss Nonno Damiano."

Love, loyalty and romance. They reap many rewards and it is the dining population of St. Louis that also benefits at Gian-Tony's.

*Photographed in Sicily is grandmother, Giovanna, and Tony's father, Damiano, at a young age.*

*The Catarinicchia family, 1960s. Back row, left to right, Tony, his mother and father, Rosaria and Damiano, and Mimma. Front row, Tony's little brother, Gian, and Giovanna.*

*Tony's uncle's engagement party in 1955. Identified in front right corner is young Tony (holding a kebab) with his sister, Mimma, at left.*

# CHICKEN CANNELLONI

INGREDIENTS
CREPES:

3 eggs

½ cup milk

2 tbsp. butter

FILLING:

4 chicken breasts

1 pkg. spinach

2 carrots

4 stalks of celery

1 sm. white onion

½ cup any white wine

SAUCE

¼ cup marinara sauce

¼ cup half & half

½ cup spinach, minced

½ cup chicken stock

Salt and pepper to taste

PESTO SAUCE:

15 leaves sweet basil

¼ cup olive oil

Crepes: Make thin egg crepes from eggs, milk, and butter.

Filling: Cook and chop spinach and chicken. Chop carrots, celery, and onions. Adding white wine and a little olive oil, blend together using a food processor to a medium consistency.

Sauce: Combine marinara sauce, half & half, minced spinach, chicken stock, salt, and pepper.

Assemble: Lay out your crepes. Add the chicken mixture and roll them up. Put the cannelloni in a pan. Pour the sauce over the crepes, covering the cannelloni. Bake at 350 degrees for approximately 12-15 minutes. Serve the cannelloni in the sauce it was baking in.

Pesto Sauce: Blend sweet basil and olive oil using a food processor. Spoon over cannelloni, if desired.

SERVES 4

# SCALLOPS CAPRICCIO

### INGREDIENTS

10 large sea scallops

¼ cup flour

¼ cup olive oil

¼ cup 40% cream

1/3 cup white wine

1/3 cup brandy

¼ cup dry vermouth

2 oz. red onions, chopped

5 oz. mushrooms

Pinch of salt

2 oz. butter

Flour and pan fry scallops until golden brown.

Sauce: Sauté chopped red onions and mushrooms in butter. Add white wine, brandy, dry vermouth, and 40% cream. Let reduce, salt to taste. Pour over scallops.

SERVES 4

*Melanzane involtini was featured on Sarah Moulton's show on the Food Network. This eggplant appetizer is one of Gian-Tony's signature dishes.*

*Sitting on the steps of St. Ambrose are, left to right, Rosario Catarinicchia, Monsignor Bommarito, Mario Batali (of the Food Network), and Tony Catarinicchia.*

*Tony has the opportunity to meet with two baseball legends from the Hill: Joe Garagiola and Yogi Berra.*

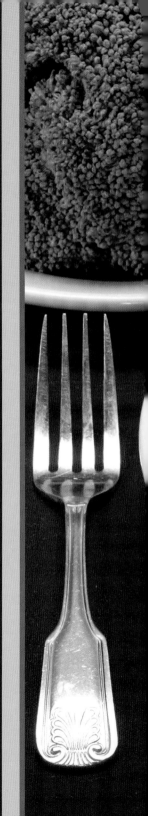

# John Mineo's

The close-knit Mineo famiglia. Back row, left to right, Cindy, John, Jr., John. Sr., and Sal. Nicholas and Anna in center front.

A bold, competitive spirit runs through the Mineo bloodline. It is this inborn resourcefulness that led John Mineo and seven of his relatives, who all started life on the same street in Palermo, Sicily, to found eight of the best Italian restaurants that St. Louis has ever seen. It is boldness such as this that led this man, less than 20 years in the United States, to start an Italian restaurant in the middle of a farm field. As yet, the beautiful homes of Town and Country were only a figment of some builder's imagination when John Mineo opened up his restaurant at the corner of Clayton and Mason in 1973. Standing in the middle of cornstalks, John's wife, Anna, reacted as many would, saying, "John, you are crazy." But Anna put her faith in her husband, and rightly so, because as it turns out, John Mineo was crazy like the proverbial fox. For 35 years later, John Mineo's Restaurant is an elegant center of delicious, inventive Italian fare in West St. Louis County.

The story of the Mineos in America began in 1956 when John Mineo's father-in-law, Paul Manno, Sr., (Anna Mineo's father) immigrated to St. Louis and by sheer good fortune was hired as a busboy by Tony and Vince Bommarito, owners of the legendary Tony's Restaurant. By 1959, things were going so well for the patriarch that all six of Paul, Sr.'s and Elena's offspring (their son, Paul, their five daughters and their husbands, all lifelong residents of a street in Palermo, Via Monte Pellegrino) followed their pioneering relative to the Gateway to the West. Also, the husbands added their names to the payroll of Tony's. To this day, the family is outspoken in their gratitude to Vince Bommarito for the wonderful start that he gave them.

Indeed, Vince Bommarito gave the Mineos, Mannos, Sanfilippos, and Gabrieles a bedrock foundation strong enough for the family members to launch, starting as early as the 1960s, the following restaurants: Agostino's (opening in 1967 at the corner of Shaw and Marconi, later to become Giovanni's), Benedetto's, GP Agostino's, J.F. Sanfilippo's, Paul Manno's, Il Bel Lago, and, of course, John Mineo's. Moreover, family loyalty does not stop at the restaurant door for this *famiglia* of restaurateurs. They are generous with each other, sharing culinary knowledge, financial support, menu ideas, and even practical help. As John Mineo says, "Even if someone is short of a dishwasher, we help each other out."

John and Anna Mineo, the co-founders of John Mineo's, certainly appreciated this well of support in the restaurant's early days when they had 12 tables and only 7 diners on Christmas Eve 1973. "Today we seat 130 for Christmas Eve, and you cannot get a reservation. Some of the original diners in 1973 now bring their children and grandchildren," says Anna.

The restaurant continues as a family affair for the Mineos. Anna has her own lunch place called Anna's that can be accessed by the side entrance of the main restaurant, while son, John, Jr., now serves as the primary manager of John Mineo's. John, Jr. exudes pride in what his par-

John, Jr. exudes pride in what his parents have accomplished, saying, "I watch my Mom and my Dad standing side by side, taking the time to carve out their own ravioli, putting in the hours and love it takes to stuff calamari perfectly. That's why our food tastes so good. It is made *con amore*."

The bold Mineo spirit is alive and well with this father and son team as both are keenly in tune with the forever changing tastes of their customers. John, Jr. explains, "My father's Mare e Monte (Sea and Mountain) pasta is a long-time favorite, yet through our menu specials we have the flexibility to add new veal choices, soft shell crabs, and Mediterranean-style dishes without interfering with traditionals like home-made cannelloni. Cooking Italian is very sim-ple, yet imaginative. We experiment with different sauces, fish, fresh vegetables, capers, and pretty soon we've created new menu specials!"

John, Jr. continues, "We are also glad to cater to our 'advanced pasta eaters.' For them we add anchovies, pine nuts, cuttlefish, and purple eggplant. We respond flexibly to special requests and sophisticated palates, especially with regard to our wine list. In the early years, it used to be lambrusco, then it was merlot and cabernet, and now it is pinot noir and good California wines which rival the French."

When asked the source of this well-spring of culinary ingenuity, John, Jr. credits his remarkable extended family, saying, "Our family get-togethers are about sharing good food, and there is also a competitive spirit on who has the best *antipasto* or *dolci*. It is about pleasing one another, which trans-lates from family members to customers."

Out of this good-natured, lifelong culinary contest the Mineos have cultivated and perfected a rare talent. As John, Jr. explains, "We have all developed this food flare and instinct. We can just walk by a platter in the dining room and with one whiff can tell if it is just right."

This Mineo gift will be shared with the rest of St. Louis at yet another location, as John and Anna's son, Paul, will soon be opening his own trattoria at Westport, thereby continuing to advance the wonderfully bold tradition born on Palermo's Via Monte Pellegrino Strada.

As an 18-year old, John Mineo served in Italy's Merchant Marine.

# SICILIAN STUFFED ARTICHOKE APPETIZER

INGREDIENTS

6 fresh artichokes, tips and thorny leaves trimmed

3 tbsp. olive oil

2 tbsp. chopped garlic

1 cup chopped fresh parsley

3 anchovies

3 cups breadcrumbs

½ cup (4 oz.) Parmigiano cheese

½ cup (4 oz.) grated Romano cheese

2 lemons

Fill large pot halfway with water. Add artichokes, placing heat-resistant plate on top to keep them in water. Cook until tender or soft. This may take 45 minutes. Drain well. Using spoon, carefully remove center petals and fuzzy centers.

In separate skillet, heat olive oil. Add garlic, parsley, anchovies, then stir in breadcrumbs and cheeses. Cook, stirring occasionally, until ingredients are dry.

Gently spread artichoke leaves and pull out center cone, scraping any purple leaves and fuzz. Fill centers and between leaves with breadcrumbs, then squeeze lemon juice over them.

SERVES 6

Married on September 24, 1957, John and Anna Mineo will be celebrating 51 years together in 2008.

114

# MARE E MONTE

INGREDIENTS

*2 tbsp. olive oil*

*2 fresh tomatoes, chopped*

*1 tbsp. chopped garlic*

*1 tbsp. chopped parsley*

*½ cup chopped fresh garlic*

*1 cup white wine*

*1 lb. fresh littleneck clams*

*2 lb. peeled and deveined shrimp*

*1 lb. lobster tail, out of shell, chopped*

*Salt and pepper to taste*

*1 lb. linguine*

In a skillet, heat olive oil with tomatoes, one tablespoon of the garlic, and parsley until hot. Add remaining garlic, wine, clams, shrimp and lobster. Season with salt and pepper. Cook, covered, until clam shells open.

In separate pot, boil water with a little salt. Cook linguine to taste. Strain. Add sauce.

SERVES 4-6

*After John and Anna married in 1957 in Palermo, they later joined her family, who had settled in St. Louis.*

*The patriarch of the Manno family, Paul Manno, Sr., as a dapper young man in Palermo, circa 1920.*

*The traditional antipasto at John Mineo's has a variety of Mediterranean delights.*

116

# Kemoll's

A desk sergeant changed Vincenzo Camuglia's name to Joe Kemoll during World War I. Little did he know that he had christened restaurant royalty.

From Castiglione, Sicily, Joe arrived alone in America in 1913 at his mother's suggestion, for there was no future for him back home. "To us," Joe's granddaughter, Ellen Cusumano, remembers, "Grandpa was warm, generous, and larger than life. Grandma [Dora], the driving force behind the business, was meticulous in her speech and comport. She never missed an opportunity to learn and improve herself–or Kemoll's."

Joe and Dora wed in 1926. When they saw a new construction on the corner of North Grand and Penrose, nine blocks north of Sportman's Park, they decided to open a new confectionery. With the bustle of Grand Avenue, it was easy to attract crowds and baseball fans alighting from the streetcars. In their new location, Dora felt compelled to expand their offerings. She asked a local Greek confectioner to teach her how to dip chocolates and make candies and he agreed. Not long after, the owner of the neighboring Zeiser Neon Signs asked that she serve lunch. She

*Restaurant royalty. Front row, left to right: Mary Grace Cusumano, JoAnn Berger, and Mary Grace's daughter, Ellen. In the back row, left to right: Mary Grace's sons, Doug and Mark.*

responded by serving plate lunches and sandwiches in addition to her candies and ices. The couple later bought the entire building, moved into an apartment upstairs, expanded into another storefront, and had two daughters, Mary Grace and JoAnn.

In 1948, while attending an Italian wedding, daughter Mary Grace met a handsome soldier in uniform and fell in love. In 1949, she married Frank Cusumano and he was joyfully accepted into the family. Dora and Joe

thought this the ideal opportunity to visit Italy and Sicily, leaving Kemoll's in the capable hands of their new son-in-law, Frank, who had a degree from St. Louis University's School of Commerce. They packed their bags, and even their Cadillac–for Joe a symbol of his success in America–for the month-long trip.

Frank's "temporary" stint at Kemoll's was successful. Over the next 40 years, he and Dora made many changes together, with Mrs. Kemoll overseeing the kitchen and dining rooms and Frank managing the business, service, and general operations. He became a partner in 1954. Frank was the sixth of nine children born in St. Louis to immigrant parents from Terrasini, Sicily. At nine years old, his mother died and he and two of his brothers were sent to St. Mary's, a Catholic boarding school in Nauvoo, Illinois. Taught by Benedictine nuns, he put his classical education to good use at Kemoll's, never failing to charm the clientele with his gentlemanly etiquette.

The Kemoll team, which now included Keith Guenther (Frank's right-hand who resembled Jack Benny) was challenged in the

'60s by a changing neighborhood and the baseball stadium moving downtown. They met the challenge by developing Gourmet Night Dinners—nine-course dinners featuring cuisine from regions in Italy, France, and other locales. The kitchen staff for Gourmet Nights always included Mrs. Kemoll and her two married daughters, JoAnn Berger and Mary Grace Cusumano. Ellen remembers her grandmother, Dora, one time unsuccessfully calling all the import stores for sorrel, needed for a French Gourmet Night. "She asked me to call Marcel and Monique Keraval, owners of the downtown Café de France, who graciously gave us the amount we needed and refused to take any money. Once, there was a brotherhood among restaurateurs, friendly competition—no one too busy to help out."

Another key to their success was Dora's meticulous and tireless efforts to only use recipes that had been tested and refined until they met her very discriminating standards. She used her mother's (née Grace Carollo Danna) Sicilian recipes, and introduced to the Midwest many dishes including calzone, cannelloni, homemade fettucine noodle dishes, and linguini con vongole.

After 62 years in the same location, guided by the fourth-generation hands of Mark, Doug, and Ellen Cusumano, Kemoll's moved in 1990 to Metropolitan Square, in the heart of downtown St. Louis. The family painstakingly duplicated the dining areas from the original. In 2003, they expanded by opening a banquet facility on the 42nd floor of Met Square, the *Top of the Met*, adding spectacular views of the city and riverfront to Kemoll's cuisine and service.

In June of 1990, only months after the family sold it, a fire consumed the old Kemoll's on North Grand. Gone forever were the beautiful oak doors with etched-glass panels, antique marble, and carved wood mantels, and brass sconces. Somehow, it felt as if a part of the family's history had been destroyed by the flames. Joe and Dora's children and grandchildren still, however, have the memories—and St. Louis, thankfully, still has Kemoll's.

Carciofi fritti *(fresh-fried artichokes) makes for a popular antipasto.*

*The original Kemoll's landmark located at 420 North Grand and Penrose.*

*Mary Grace and JoAnn Kemoll have an outing to the Fox Theatre.*

*Joe Kemoll, in 1940, during his pre-pink Cadillac era.*

# FILET DOUGLAS

INGREDIENTS

*1 cup Cognac*

*1 cup (16 oz.) heavy whipping cream*

*½ cup prepared cream sauce*

*1 tbsp. red wine vinegar*

*1½ tsp. salt*

*½ tsp. white pepper*

*2 (6 oz. each) cold-water lobster*

*4 (4 oz. each) filet mignon*

*Salt, pepper and extra-virgin olive oil*

*Chopped fresh parsley or other green garnish*

In a small sauce pan, heat Cognac over medium heat. With extreme caution, using an extended reach lighter, ignite it to burn off the alcohol. This takes 1 or 2 minutes. Add cream, cream sauce (several excellent sauces with Parmesan cheese in them are available at the Italian grocery stores around St. Louis), vinegar, salt, and pepper. Continue to simmer over low heat, stirring occasionally.
Set aside.

Prepare lobster by splitting tail down middle and removing meat from both halves. Rinse thoroughly. Cut into 6 pieces per tail. Pat dry, using paper towel. Reserve in refrigerator.

Rub beef with a little oil and salt and pepper. Cook by grilling or pan-searing. For stovetop preparation, heat teaspoon of oil in a skillet. Sear meat, one filet at a time. Cook until almost the desired temperature. Drain oil and add pre-made sauce and lobster. Continue to cook over medium heat until lobster has just finished cooking.

On platter, serve filet mignon and lobster with sauce. Garnish with parsley.

SERVES 4

120

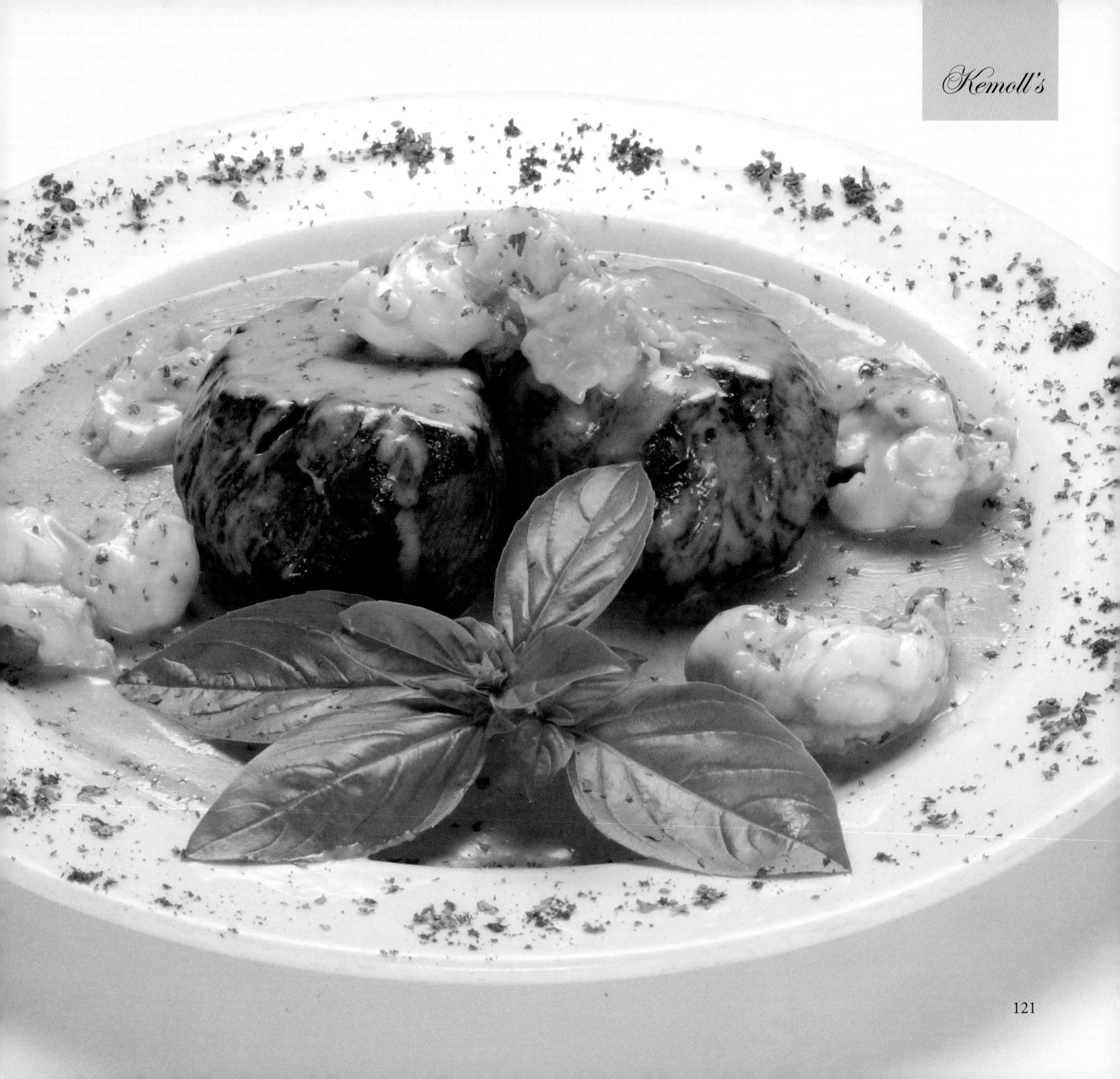

*The new Florentine room was unveiled in the 1960s.*

*The Kemoll/Cusumano team greet guests in front of their North Grand entrance.*

# SHRIMP ARTICHOKE MOUTARDE

INGREDIENTS

*2 medium fresh artichokes*

*drawn butter*

*¾ cup heavy whipping cream*

*½ cup cream sauce (flavored with*
  *Parmesan cheese)*

*¼ cup Dijon mustard*

*2 tbsp. dried tarragon leaves*

*12 fresh shrimp (preferably 8 to 10 per pound),*
  *peeled and deveined, tail still attached*

Butterfly shrimp down middle three-fourths of the way. Rinse thoroughly and pat dry with paper towel. Refrigerate.

Peel artichokes down to the heart, or use canned, quartered, artichoke hearts. Steam leaves. Serve with drawn butter for appetizer.

Use peeler on stem section, then quarter the whole bottom and remove pith. Cut in thin slices. Drop into boiling water, with lemon juice added, for 2 minutes. Immediately dunk in bowl of ice water until cool. Dry with paper towels. Hold in lemon water for later use.

In medium skillet, heat cream, cream sauce, Dijon mustard, tarragon and shrimp. Bring to simmer. Add artichokes. Reduce to low and cook just until shrimp is done.

Serve on platter.

SERVES 4

*Dora and Joe Kemoll enjoy an opportunity to let others do the cooking.*

*Dora Kemoll was always experimenting to expand the Kemoll's menu. Her granddaughter, Ellen, still cherishes "precious moments in which working alongside Grandma Dora was a joy and privilege for me everyday."*

122

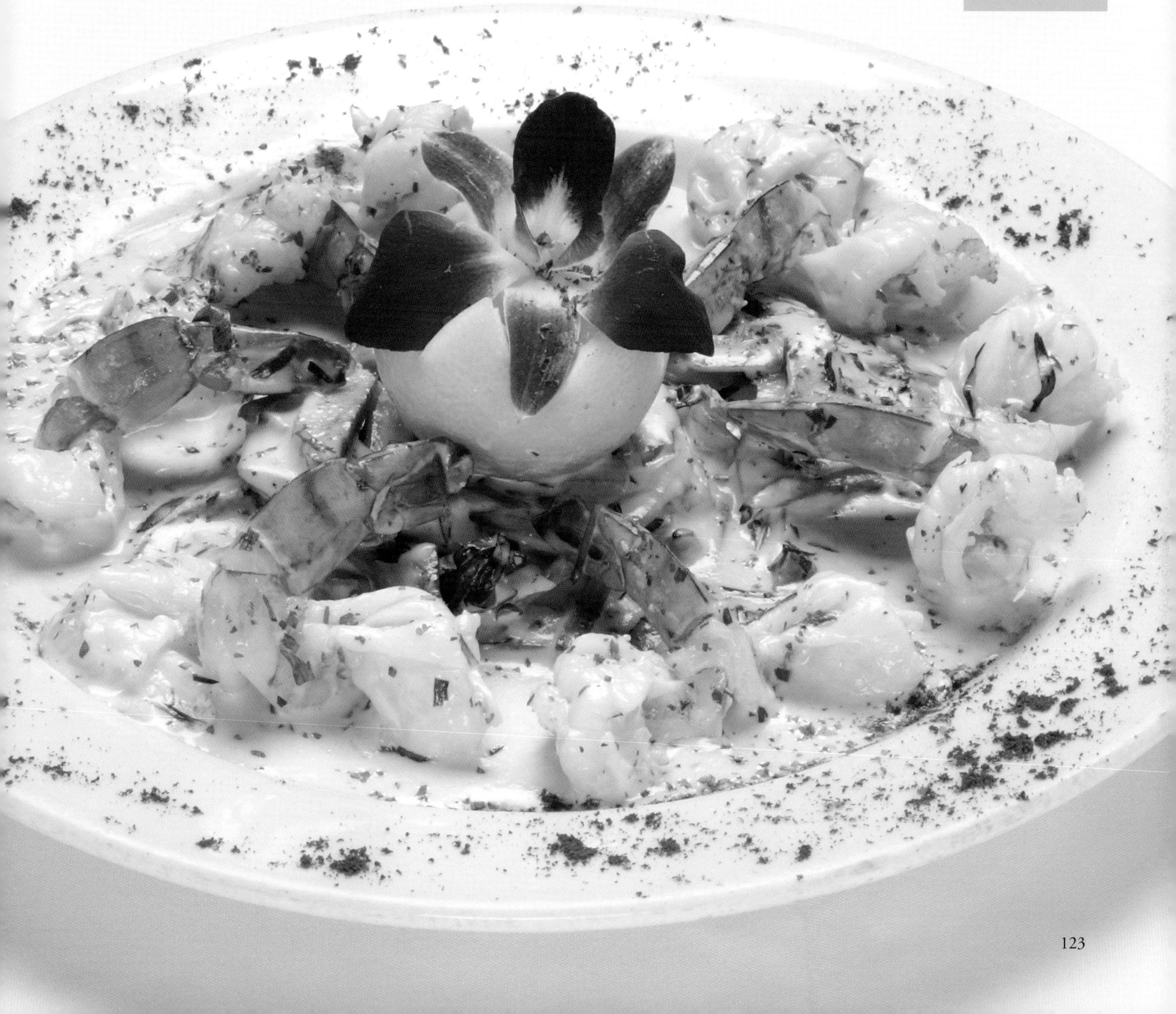

# Lombardo's

From a fruit and vegetable stand to serving the President of the United States: that is the amazing story of Lombardo's.

As in the case with many of the great Italian restaurants of St. Louis, it all started on the Mediterranean island of Sicily, when the grandparents made the journey across the Atlantic in the late 1800s, settling in St. Louis.

Angelo Lombardo, Sr. opened a fruit stand in 1929 at Riverview and West Florissant. In 1934, during the Great Depression, he expanded by building a small restaurant. The restaurant was operated by his brother, Gus, his sisters, Michaela and Sue, and his oldest son, Gus. Angelo and Anna's children, Gus, Lee, Tom, Angelo, Jr., and Carmen helped in the business. Carmen and Angelo remember sorting soda bottles for return deposit after school. Angelo, Sr. encouraged his sons to follow their own path. His son, Tom, certainly did (see page 20).

By the 1960s, companies like General Motors, Emerson Electric, Combustion Eng., Mallinckrodt, and several small businesses had offices and plants in North St. Louis, thereby creating a need for a fine dining establishment. In 1965, the Lombardo family responded by tearing down their old produce stand and restaurant and building an upscale facility. Brothers Gus, Angelo, Jr., and Carmen managed the new restaurant and their sister, Lee, helped gather the family recipes originally created by the aunts and their mother, Anna. Lee also served as the cashier for several years.

*Karen Lombardo Baker stands in between her father, Carmen (on her right), and her Uncle Angelo.*

During the 1960s, 1970s, and 1980s, the elegant Lombardo's became a mainstay for business people and residents of North County and several other areas.

In addition to excellent service, great food, and a central location, Lombardo's now famous toasted ravioli also played an important role in bringing prosperity to this family business. "Our boiled ravioli in the 1930s and our toasted ravioli from the 1940s were uniquely crescent-shaped, not the usual St. Louis-style square," Angelo, Jr. explains. "To this day they are cut with a round cookie cutter. We serve our ravioli with white or red sauce, and sometimes use green dough or spinach filling. The combinations are endless."

After so many years in the business, Angelo, Jr. and Carmen have seen the world of food transition. "Tastes change," says Angelo, "Once short ribs and kraut, chicken and dumplings were the comfort foods. You can't give them away today!" The brothers also remember that, in the 1960s, there weren't boneless chicken breasts on restaurant menus. "That came in the 1970s," Carmen says, "when the lunch crowd could not get enough of Jack Salmon, fried shrimp, and fried oysters. We could get our trout and catfish from a number of local suppliers, but for salmon, shrimp, and oysters, Meletio's was the only place to go, because back in the 1950s, there was no such thing as fresh fish flown in like there is today."

Carmen, remembering the smaller, more confined kitchens of yesteryear, says, "Back then we were our own butchers, carving up a leg of veal, which weighed 135 pounds, or a side of beef at 400 pounds. Consequently, we had a very small prep room."

Not to be outdone by generations past, Carmen's children, Michael, Anthony, and Karen, set out on their own in 1991 and opened Lombardo's Trattoria in the Drury Inn next to Union Station. Just one year later, the younger Lombardos had the honor of serving President George H.W. Bush, his family, and members of the Cabinet following his 1992 debate with then Governor Bill Clinton at Washington University. However, around the same time, many of the businesses that had brought so many customers to the original Lombardo's began to close their doors or move their facilities to other parts of the St. Louis metropolitan area. As a result, Carmen and Angelo, Jr., still the general managers, knew they had to make a radical change if they were to survive.

Once again, by creating another partnership with Charles and Shirley Drury, owners of the Drury Inn Corporation, Angelo, Jr. and Carmen breathed new life into the Lombardo's brand. By 1993, the original Lombardo's had moved to a beautiful new facility near Lambert Airport, which has become a favorite for, not only local businesspeople, but for brides and grooms and others wishing to celebrate in Lombardo's excellent banquet facilities. The brothers express their gratitude to the Drurys for providing the help and expertise needed to assist the family in this new, exciting chapter of the business.

Indeed, in August of 2000, the Lombardo-Drury partnership reached a whole new level when Anthony and Michael Lombardo opened yet another stellar Lombardo family restaurant. Carmine's Steak House, located in the heart of downtown St. Louis and Lombardo's Trattoria in the new Drury Inn, west of Union Station.

A century ago, Angelo, Sr. set up a modest fruit and vegetable stand in North St. Louis with the hope that his family could live a decent life in America. Today, his children and grandchildren preside over some excellent St. Louis restaurants. Beginning with a humble fruit stand, Angelo set his family on the path to living that elusive promise made to so many immigrants, the American Dream.

# ITALIAN SAUSAGE A LA LOMBARDO

### INGREDIENTS

*2 tbsp. margarine or butter*

*2 oz. green bell pepper, sliced julienne*

*2 oz. onion, sliced julienne*

*2 whole tomatoes, peeled, sliced julienne*

*¼ cup sherry wine*

*¼ cup beef or veal stock*

*Cooked linguine or pasta of choice*

*Italian sausage links, broiled or grilled*

*Chopped fresh parsley*

In skillet, melt margarine. Cook green bell peppers, onion, and tomatoes, stirring often, until al dente. Drain. Add wine, then stock. Continue to cook until heated thoroughly. Add cooked pasta of choice.

To serve, place pasta mixture in bowl. Top with sausage. Sprinkle with parsley.

SERVES 1

*Photo Above: In 1934, Lombardo's Tavern was added next to the fruit stand visible on the left at Riverview and West Florissant.*

*Photo Below: By the 1950s, Lombardo's Tavern had expanded into a local landmark restaurant.*

*Brother Gus, relaxing in this 1960 photo, has proved to be the cornerstone of the Lombardo team from the 1930s till 1995.*

126

*In 1965, Lombardo's went upscale with this elegant new facility.*

*Tom Lombardo "The Spark Plug" of Soldan High School, West Point, and war hero, won the Italian-American National Award. Full story on page 20.*

# VEAL SALTIMBOCCA

INGREDIENTS

8 oz. veal cutlet, thinly sliced

2 thin slices (1 oz. each) Provel cheese

2 thin slices (1 oz. each) prosciutto ham

Flour

6 tbsp. butter

¼ cup white wine

¼ cup veal stock

½ cup (2 oz.) grated Romano cheese

Chopped fresh parsley

Pound veal even thinner. Place cheese and prosciutto on half a piece of veal. Fold over to form pocket. Flour exterior lightly.

In skillet, melt butter. Cook veal pocket over medium heat 4 minutes on each side. Drain. Add wine and stock. Sprinkle with cheese. Simmer 2 minutes.

To serve, sprinkle with a little parsley.

SERVES 1-2

*Above: Lombardo's Tuscan specialty crostini. At right: Fountains and chandeliers in the 1965 facility.*

# *Lorenzo's*

*Larry with his lovely wife,
Maureen, and their two girls,
Audrey (on the left) and Claudia.*

If he could, Larry Fuse, Jr. would make two more copies of himself. One Larry would run his successful eatery, Lorenzo's Trattoria, (established in October, 1999), another would stay home and spend every moment with his wife, Maureen, and their two girls, 6-year old Claudia and 4-year old Audrey. The third Larry would be out on the golf course, trying to beat Tiger's score on a bad day. However, since he can't, he'll have to do what his parents and grandparents have always done: do it all. And very successfully, we might add.

Ever since he was a young boy on Sublette, Larry's dream was food. Not just eating it, but creating with it. "My grandparents and their family emigrated from Cuggiono, Italy. One of my most vivid memories was watching my grandma and her sisters cooking all the big, Italian meals for the holidays–homemade ravioli, sauce, polenta, and rustita. I remember in particular how excited I was to be allowed to make the ravioli, rolling out the dough and working alongside my grandma and great-aunt, who are masters in the kitchen."

Larry realized his dream, but he had to travel up the ranks. After graduating from CBC High School in 1994, he earned a degree in Culinary Arts from Forest Park Community College in 1998. "I first learned the simplest tasks by working in Hill kitchens cleaning vegetables and doing prep work. My first cooking

job was at Brazie's Restaurant, after that a 2-year apprenticeship at St. Louis Country Club, then Café Mira in Clayton." And after that, he founded Lorenzo's at the ripe, old age of 23.

Since his father and partner owned the building that houses his restaurant, as well as running a construction company, Larry, Jr. was able to create his space according to his specifications. He wanted to make sure diners enjoyed their food in a backdrop of walls of windows complemented by a soft, modern palette of light pastels, which is also easy on the palate. A light, roomy bar invites lingering and lounging either before or after a meal. Add to that a loyal staff, most of whom have been with the Trattoria since its opening. But the food, oh the food…

Where to begin? Lorenzo's is a fusion of Northern Italian with surprising touches of contemporary flavors. From the kitchen, emanates the aroma of homemade gnocchi, risotto, braised ossobuco and the restaurant's specialty, chicken spiedini. The bruschetta bursts with chunks of caramelized onions, Asiago cheese, and pale tomatoes topped with basil herb. The shrimp scampi is presented like a work of art on a bed of roasted peppers with white beans and lemon aioli. The wines are the best that California and Italian vineyards have to offer.

Larry's family loyalty has always been on the Hill. "My grandfather worked at the famous Ruggeri's Restaurant, which at one time seemed to cater to half of the St. Louis dining population. Grandpa's passion for food preparation was also an inspiration to me. I also remember when my Dad would make chicken risotto with saffron chicken liver, gizzards and chicken meat. It took all day to make the chicken stock and put all the ingredients together, but it was so good and he was very proud. Early in the morning my dad would go to Marconi Bakery to buy dough, let it rise, form doughnuts and fry them. Then we'd slather them with butter and jelly and coat them with sugar. What a delicious memory."

The chef-owner of Lorenzo's Trattoria has no regrets about his choice of a life. He works hard, is devoted to his family and extended family but it is his kitchen that is his demanding and exacting mistress. "I love waking up every day, heading out the door where my kitchen awaits. Here I am allowed to create delectable dinners for my appreciative clientele by creating new looks and new tastes. Pleasing them is the cornerstone of my personal philosophy on service."

Come to think of it, maybe <u>one</u> of Larry Fuse, Jr. is just enough to go around.

131

# RICOTTA CHEESECAKE

### CRUST

1 lb. flour (about 4 cups)
1 cup sugar
Pinch of salt
¼ lb. (1 stick) butter, cubed
2 eggs
1 tsp. milk
1 tsp. vanilla

### FILLING

1½ lb. Ricotta cheese
1½ lb. cream cheese
2 cups sugar
15 whole eggs
Zest and juice of 1 orange
¾ tbsp. vanilla

### CRUST

Combine flour, sugar, and salt in food processor. Blend in butter until grainy. Add eggs, milk, and vanilla. Whirl until mixture forms a ball. Remove dough from food processor. Knead with a little more flour until it becomes firmer. Roll out to fit in two (9-inch) spring form pans. Cut a round piece of parchment paper to fit on top and place over the crusts. Weight them with something like white beans. Bake in a preheated 350-degree oven 20 to 30 minutes.

### FILLING

In large mixer bowl, combine both Ricotta and cream cheese and sugar. Mix on high speed of electric mixer until smooth. Add orange zest and juice and vanilla. Mix well. Add eggs, 3 at a time, incorporated fully before adding more. When crust is done, wrap bottom and sides of pan with aluminum foil to avoid leakage. Divide filling between pans and place in hot water bath (larger pan of hot water). Bake in preheated 325-degree oven about 1-1/2 hours. Remove from oven. Let cool.

*Pasqualina and John Manzelli are great grandparents to Larry Fuse, Jr. They were married circa 1910.*

*Grandparents to Larry Fuse, Jr., John and Jenny Fuse were married in 1949.*

John Fuse and coworker, circa 1955, at St. Louis' most popular restaurant at the time, Ruggeri's.

Larry's grandfather, John Fuse, makes a martini at the famous Ruggeri's bar.

Seated from left: Larry's aunt and uncle, Patty and Steve Ringkamp; Larry's parents, Sandy and Larry Fuse, Sr. Standing is Grandma Jenny Fuse.

# GNOCCHI

INGREDIENTS

*3 large Idaho potatoes, peeled, quartered*

*1 egg, beaten*

*1 tsp. salt*

*¼ tsp. pepper*

*8 oz. fresh spinach, cooked, well drained and chopped*

*2 tbsp. olive oil*

*¼ cup grated Parmesan cheese*

*2 cups flour*

In large saucepan, add enough water to cover potatoes. Bring water to boil. Cook until fork-tender. Pour potatoes into strainer and shake to drain any excess water. Place potatoes on baking sheet and bake in a preheated 350-degree oven for about 10 minutes or until potatoes are dry.

While potatoes are still hot, pass them through a potato ricer or food mill into large bowl. Make small well in the middle of potatoes. Pour egg into well. Add salt, pepper, spinach and olive oil. Sprinkle cheese over potato. Add about 1½ cups of flour. Knead dough, using both hands, until firm. Add more flour as needed. It should only take 3 to 4 minutes to form the dough; it is important to not over-work it. Cut dough in sections and roll it into ropes about ½-inch thick. Gently roll back of a fork (or a gnocchi board) over dough to form ridges. Dough pieces should be about ½-inch long

Cook the gnocchi in a pot of boiling salted water. Place dough in the water in batches and stir gently to keep gnocchi from sticking together. When they start floating to the top, immediately remove them. Top them with a favorite sauce and serve immediately.

SERVES 6

135

# LoRusso's Cucina

*The ever-popular host and hostess, Rich and Terri of LoRusso's Cucina.*

If you look up "mosaic" in the dictionary, you will get words such as *variety, mixture, assortment,* and *mixed bag.* No words could more aptly describe the life and times of Terri and Rich LoRusso. Add to that the adjectives, *congenial* and *entertaining,* then you've got the picture.

Though Rich was born and raised on the Hill and dutifully attended good schools like Sacred Heart Villa, St. Ambrose and Southwest High, he was often kicked out of classes for his clownish antics. Consequently, it took him a while longer to graduate. Deciding to press his nose to the grindstone, the young man toiled as a "salad boy" at Godfather's Ristorante for seven years and, over time, Rich worked his way up to head chef. However, he could not concentrate on the lettuce as his eyes kept travelling to the face and figure of the new "bus-girl." In order to keep her admirer from chopping off his fingers, Terri had no other choice but to marry him.

When the place closed, Rich felt adrift, complained to his wife, so she advised, "Quit moping, get out there and start your own business!" Thus in 1986, LoRusso's Italian Café was born and it flourished. A 9-table establishment, it soon became apparent that it was bursting at the seams (or maybe it was Rich's brand of humorous hosting that drew in the crowds). Saying farewell to the neighborhood, the couple moved the business to its current spot on Watson and Arsenal.

Wife Terri remembers, "The late 1980s were our young and ambitious years. Back then we ran the Nanna LoRusso Bakery on the Hill, Tutto Bene in West County, LoRussos on the Hill as well as raising two children under three while gutting and revamping our home." As if that wasn't enough, they decided to expand their boundaries. Purchasing the neighboring furniture repair store in 2005, they added more space. Rich, as well as his comedic and entrepreneurial skills, developed a collector's eye for antiques and period art. He decorated his banquet room with Chihuly-inspired glass while the restaurant and bar are adorned with Toulouse Lautrec poster art and displays of vintage advertising such as Campari Bottlers.

Even the menu is a mixture of Sicilian and modern. Take for example, the scampi a la spinachi (spinach and spicy lobster sauce) –very unique. The house-made tortellini and ravioli are stuffed full of crab meat or spinach. If you want excitement, their colorful cioppino has devotees as far away as New York and San Francisco firmly declaring it the best they've ever tasted.

Not to out-do themselves, Rich and Terri are now bottling their own wine. Of course, they had to go to the source, so they visited the internationally-acclaimed vineyard, Au Bon Climat, spending quality time barrel-tasting and selecting Barbera and a Pinot Grigio Blend, to be made only for them in a special patch of the California vineyard. "We are seeing more trends in Super Tuscan blends such as Luce gaining in popularity as well as Tignanello," the wine-experts inform.

Can this super-duo stretch themselves any further? Yes they can and do so by giving tirelessly to charitable foundations and donating of their time and efforts. The ones closest to their hearts are the Lupus Foundation and Logos School in Olivette.

The class clown, along with his devoted

audience of one, Terri, have garnered and deserved a plethora of accolades. The Missouri House of Representatives passed a resolution saluting Rich LoRusso's life and work. In 2004, he was named Restaurateur of the Year. But what makes him so proud is the Zagat survey listing their restaurant as one of the best Italian eateries in St. Louis. "The fact that it wasn't produced by paid critics but by independent volunteers makes it all the more meaningful."

Just keep doing what you're doing, you two. Entertain us, surprise us, delight us with your energy, talent, kindness, friendliness, and mouth-watering cuisine. The Hill and St. Louis will never tire of you.

*Part of Rich's beloved rooster collection.*

# CIOPPINO

### INGREDIENTS

1 tbsp. (or more) chopped garlic

1/3 cup chopped red onion (plus 1/4 cup chopped
    celery and carrot, if desired)

2 tbsp. (packed) chopped fresh basil

10 turns freshly ground black pepper

2 pinches crushed red pepper flakes

½ cup Chianti wine

1 can (28 oz.) chopped plum tomatoes

1 tsp. lobster or shrimp base dissolved
    in 1 cup water (or clam juice)

2 tbsp. chopped fresh parsley

Salt to taste

½ tsp. saffron

8 large sea scallops

4 extra-large shrimp

8 oz. swordfish, tuna or other firm fish

8 fresh whole clams

12 green lip mussels

½ cup arborio rice

Extra clam juice

Italian bread, sliced

*Christmas in 1924 on the Hill. Grandpa Vincenzo LoRusso who, in 1913, married Serafina. She holds Joe, Rich's father.*

*La Famiglia; Father and son, Rich and Joe Lo Russo.*

*Off to the piazza for the May Crowning Festival at Sacred Heart Villa, which early brought out Rich's showmanship.*

In large skillet, cook and stir garlic, onion, basil, black pepper and red pepper until onion is transparent. Add wine. Heat and stir to loosen pieces of mixture from bottom of skillet. Add undrained tomatoes, dissolved liquid, parsley and salt. Simmer, covered, 10 minutes. Add saffron, scallops, shrimp, swordfish, clams, mussels, and rice. Cook over medium heat, covered, adding hot clam juice, ½ cup at a time, until rice is desired texture and seafood is cooked thoroughly.

Serve in bowls, with Italian bread on the side.

SERVES 2

138

*Tom and Barbara keep little brother, Rich, out of trouble.*

*Meeting at Godfather's Ristorante, Rich and Terri soon tied the knot.*

*As one class-clown to another in 1982, Red Skelton is greeted by Rich, Terri, and Jimmy LoRusso.*

# CRAWFISH AND ANDOUILLE FETTUCCINE

*The winner is: this recipe. LoRusso's Cucina, in 1998, inaugurated the Pasta Bowl in which customers, at Super Bowl season, select the best new pasta dish submitted by a local cook. Each time the winning dish is served, the LoRussos contribute $2 to Operation Food Search. To date, they have raised $40,000.*

INGREDIENTS

| | |
|---|---|
| *1 lb. fettuccine* | *2 tbsp. sweet basil* |
| *¼ cup extra virgin olive oil* | *½ tsp. thyme* |
| *¼ cup finely chopped bell peppers* | *1½ tsp. salt* |
| *½ cup finely chopped green onions* | *½ tsp. white pepper* |
| *½ cup finely chopped celery* | *¼ tsp. black pepper* |
| *1½ tbsp. minced garlic* | *¼ tsp. cayenne pepper* |
| *1 lb. crawfish tails with fat* | *½ pint whipping cream* |
| *½ lb. finely chopped andouille sausage* | *7 tbsp. grated imported Romano cheese* |
| *2 tbsp. Italian seasoning* | *2 tbsp. finely chopped parsley* |
| *1 tsp. ground oregano* | |

Boil a pound of fettuccine noodles al dente. Heat the olive oil until hot and sauté the bell peppers, green onions, celery, and garlic until slightly softened. Don't burn the garlic!

Next add the crawfish tails and andouille sausage over medium heat for 3 to 5 minutes and blend well with the vegetables. Be sure to stir constantly during these 3 to 5 minutes. Natural juices will form at the bottom of the pan. As soon as these juices begin to sizzle sprinkle in the dry ingredients (Italian seasoning, oregano, basil, and thyme) over the crawfish and andouille and stir them in well.

Add your 3 different peppers (white, black, cayenne) and the salt and work them into the blend. Taste the "gravy" at this point and see if any adjustments are needed and cook for about 2 more minutes.

Remove the crawfish from the pan so they don't overcook. At this point start slowly adding the whipping cream and stir constantly as you pour. Crank the heat back up to high and cook until it begins to thicken (probably about 7 minutes).

Return the crawfish to the pan and turn the heat down to low and gradually add the fettuccine into the sauce. Stir the pasta so all the noodles are coated with the sauce and simmer for about one minute so the pasta is reheated.

Serve in a pasta bowl topped with Romano cheese and parsley.

SERVES 6

# The Pasta House Co.

*The affable and gregarious Kim Tucci.*

Kim Tucci is truly a man for all seasons… Restaurateur, political advisor, ex-maitre d', ex-high school teacher and coach, ex-college teacher, stock broker, auctioneer, and would-be priest. (Not to mention bartender, parking lot attendant, disc jockey, trainer, and advertising executive.)

Today, Kim is president of the very-successful and popular Pasta House Co. To the many charitable organizations he supports, he is a hero. One may well ask the question: What makes a hero who is also the recipient of so much success? How did all the awards and accolades come about? How does one become such a hero?

Kim Tucci is quick to tell you that, for him, it begins with the great gifts he received from his immigrant grandparents Virginia and Roberto, his uncle Lorenzo, and his mother and father. They gave him unconditional love and a set of values, which include an understanding of the simple difference between right and wrong and the importance of having a strong work ethic.

Kim grew up in North St. Louis. He lived in a small apartment above his grandfather's store in Walnut Park, known as Little Hill. Even as a young boy he marveled at the hours his grandfather spent working in his grocery store. Kim helped him make salsiccia every Thursday night in order to have them ready to be delivered to customers the next day.

His father, Alfred Tucci, was a police officer. Whenever Kim speaks about his father, it is with reverence. "He was perfect. He was a great policeman, a great athlete, the most respected man in the neighborhood. He even worked weekends as an umpire picking up $7.50 a game. My Dad would come home exhausted. But he did it for us!"

Tucci's father never lectured nor preached to his son. He never had to because his non-verbal behavior was perfectly clear. He never doubted his father's strong moral code.

It was for this reason Kim decided to be the best he could be. And not only that, to give back to society whatever success he attained. His success in the popular Pasta House Co. reflects those precepts.

Along with partner, Joe Fresta and late partner, John Ferrara, Tucci founded The Pasta House Co. restaurant chain more than 34 years ago. Serving five million diners a year at 32 locations, their system of community involvement and market saturation is an ongoing, extremely successful strategy. So much so they've expanded to other states like Illinois, Kentucky, and even an international franchise in the Dominican Republic.

As to community outreach, the chain and the Coco-Cola Corporation established "Reading, Writing and Ravioli" as well as its "Great Works of Art High School Contest," which offer college scholarships for talented high school students. Through the Caring and Sharing Program, over five thousand St. Louisans are fed every Christmas. Seeing the strong need, not just during the holiday season, Tucci and his partner assist families in need all year round.

The list of accolades for this man are endless and appreciation for his involvement bottomless. Just to name a few, Tucci was awarded Man of the Year more than 20 times, Missouri Restaurateur of the Year, the prestigious Catholic Youth Council Silver Boot, the Dr. Martin Luther King, Jr. Distinguished Community/ Civic Service Award and he was also selected as one of the Top 100 Business Leaders in the St. Louis Region.

Need we say more?

Well, maybe this: Kim Tucci believes that the way to a patron's heart is through honest communication so his company developed the 'Bend Over Backwards' program. The focus is on making sure that both employee and clientele are on the same page when it comes to satisfaction, safety, and making sure his restaurants are the friendliest in the state, in the nation and even in the world.

But, to Kim, what is most important is that he has successfully followed in the footsteps of his parents and grandparents. Looking at all he has done and how he has gone about it, he can trust in the fact that he has gone above and beyond their expectations. For those of us who have benefited from his gifts and largesse, St. Louis can honestly say, "He did it for us!"

The scrumptious desert tray is always a tempting choice at The Pasta House Co.

Kim's immigrant grandfather, Roberto Tucci is photographed minding the store in 1954.

Back row: Left to right, Eugene Tucci, Virginia Tucci, and Larry Tucci. Front row: Phyllis Tegethoff and J. Kim Tucci.

# CHICKEN SPIEDINI

INGREDIENTS

*2 (6 oz. each) chicken breasts*

*Vinaigrette dressing (¼ cup per serving)*

*Dry seasoned breadcrumbs*

*1 cup white wine-lemon-butter sauce, divided*
  *(purchased or prepared)*

*½ cup fresh sliced mushrooms*

*1/3 cup grated Provel and Mozzarella cheese (combined)*

*Chopped fresh parsley*

Cut each chicken breast into 8 pieces and place on 8-inch stainless steel skewer. Marinate in vinaigrette, covered, in refrigerator at least 4 hours. Remove skewers from marinade and roll in breadcrumbs, without packing or over-breading. Broil until cooked thoroughly.

In small skillet, heat lemon-butter sauce. Add mushrooms to sauce until cooked thoroughly.

Preheat oven to 350 degrees. Place spiedini in baking dish and remove skewers. Top with cheese. Heat in preheated oven until cheese melts.

To serve, top spiedini evenly with mushrooms and sauce. Garnish with chopped parsley.

White Wine-Lemon-Butter Sauce: Bring ¼ cup lemon juice and ¼ cup dry white wine to boil over medium heat. Continue to heat, stirring often, until reduced by one-third. Add ¼ cup heavy cream. Simmer 3 to 4 minutes until mixture thickens. Slowly add 1 cup (2 sticks) butter until completely incorporated. Season with salt, pepper, granular garlic, dash of pepper sauce, and dried parsley to taste.

SERVES 2

*Featured decoration at the restaurant is a selection of movie posters with Italian films and American films whose title is translated into Italian.*

144

*Left to right: Joe Fresta, John Ferrara, and Kim Tucci, Pasta House Co. partners in 1998.*

*Photo Above: Shown, left to right, are Larry, Frank, Al (Kim's father), Eugene Tucci in 1933. Al was a policeman whom Kim greatly admired and emulates in his professional life to this day.*

*Photo Left: Kim Tucci is being held by his uncle, Jack Neusel, in 1943.*

# MEDITERRANEAN SEAFOOD PASTA

### INGREDIENTS

*2 tbsp. extra-virgin olive oil*

*6 pieces red bell pepper flakes*

*2 anchovies, chopped*

*¼ cup diced yellow onion*

*1 tsp. minced garlic*

*1 tsp. capers*

*7 Kalamata olives*

*5 to 7 oz. whitefish, cut in 5 pieces*

*4 shrimp (16 to 20 per lb.)*

*¾ cup marinara or tomato sauce, heated*

*8 oz. linguine*

*2 to 4 fresh basil leaves*

*chopped fresh parsley*

Heat olive oil. Cook red pepper, anchovies, onion, garlic, capers, and olives, stirring often, for 1 minute. Add fish and shrimp. Cook, stirring constantly, 1 minute longer. Add marinara sauce. Cook, covered, 2 minutes or until fish is thoroughly cooked.

Cook linguine according to package directions. Add with fresh basil to sauce. Garnish with parsley.

SERVES 2

*Longtime friends and partners (left to right), Joe Fresta and Kim Tucci are photographed in 2007.*

146

The Pasta House Co.

# Paul Manno's

*Cooking is a family affair with the Mannos. Paul, Jr. is flanked between his parents, Concetta and Paul, Sr.*

It is a typical Friday night. At 5 p.m., Paul, Jr. has already prepped the kitchen and consulted Mama Concetta. Lights are dimmed and Frank Sinatra, "Ol' Blue Eyes," plays softly in the background. In the best Sicilian tradition, father and son line up at the door to greet the first of their customers. From the kitchen emanates the aromatic scent of garlic and tomato sauce stirred by Mama Concetta, who had been working hard all afternoon. If you are very lucky, not only will you enjoy the warmth and charm of Papa Manno, he might just serenade you with his best Venetian-gondolier version of *O Solo Mio*.

Paul, Sr. likes to tell the story of how his hidden gem came into being. "In 1956, I came here with my father to visit my sick grandmother who had immigrated to St. Louis in 1900. I met her for the first time at 17 and liked the city so much I stayed." By 1959, he and his father earned enough money to send for his 5 sisters. Their husbands launched what became John Mineo's, Agostino's and Giovanni's, but it was Paul, Sr.'s 14-year stint as dining room director at Tony's ("the restaurant innovator of us all") that gave him the professional push he needed. At age 41, he partnered with his brother-in-law to open the doors of John Mineo and Paul's at 515 North 6th Street in downtown St. Louis. Striking out on his own, Paul, Sr. opened a restaurant in St. Charles. However, it was tougher during that era as Italian food did not enjoy the popularity that it does today.

Following in Papa Manno's footsteps is his son, Paul, Jr. While still a junior at UMSL, he received a phone call from his father–Massa's at the Forum Shopping Center in Chesterfield was selling. Would he be interested in opening his own restaurant? The answer was a resounding, "Yes." Totally trusting in his 21-year-old son's instincts and skills, Paul, Sr. bought the facility, confident that his first-class family apprenticeship would see his son succeed. Reflecting over the last 13 years, Paul, Jr. smiles with pride. "All I ever wanted to do was own my own restaurant, working alongside my parents." Nowadays, though, Paul, Sr. likes to spend a lot of time with his daughter, a university professor in Ragusa, Sicily, or talking with his grandchildren on the Internet.

148

Paul, Jr. has intentionally kept the place small and intimate. Even buying the barber shop next door merely expanded the place by five tables. Also, the Mannos keep the menu mainly classic, with emphasis on Southern Italian fare of fish, lemon, spices, and tomatoes (as opposed to northern cuisine featuring risotto, polenta, and cream sauce).

Paul, Jr. reveals that the secret to a successful enterprise is taking care of people. "National accolades will come your way but nothing beats the smile and gratitude of a contented, happy customer."

The famed Zagat restaurant survey advises, "Skip the Hill," and head to the Chesterfield strip mall at Woods Mill and Olive to taste the best Sicilian fare. "Just like mama used to make because mama is still in the kitchen."

*Married in 1965, Paul Manno, Sr. and his wife, Concetta, celebrate their 43rd anniversary.*

# RIGATONI ARRABIATA

### INGREDIENTS

8 oz. rigatoni noodles

1 tbsp. extra virgin olive oil

½ cup sliced mushrooms

1 cup chopped tomatoes

1 tsp. capers

3 chopped green olives

¼ cup sherry wine

1 tsp. red pepper flakes

2 cups tomato sauce

Salt and pepper to taste

Parmigiano cheese

Bring a large pot of water to boil. Add salt and rigatoni. Cook the pasta al dente.

Meanwhile, heat the oil in a large skillet. Saute the mushrooms, capers, and green olives. Add the chopped tomatoes, red pepper flakes, and sherry wine. Add tomato sauce. Season with salt and pepper and cook for 10 minutes. Mix drained pasta into the sauce and serve with grated Parmigiano.

SERVES 2

On the night Denzel Washington (photo below with Paul, Jr.) came to the restaurant, the patrons enjoyed an unexpected surprise which they will long remember.

Left to right: Ozzie Smith, Charlie Steiner, on the right and Joe Torre, and Bob Gibson flank Paul, Jr. on the left.

Paul Manno's

151

# VEAL PANNA

### INGREDIENTS

*2 tbsp. butter*

*1 tbsp. finely chopped onion*

*6 slices baby veal, pounded thin*

*½ cup flour*

*1 cup chopped mushrooms*

*½ cup sherry wine*

*1 cup heavy whipping cream*

*Salt and pepper to taste*

    Melt butter in skillet. Add onion. Coat veal with flour and cook with onion until lightly browned on both sides. Add mushrooms and sherry. Cook 1 minute. Add heavy cream. Cook until cream is reduced by half. Season with salt and pepper.

SERVES 3

*One of St. Louis' most well-known sports' broadcasters, Joe Buck, poses for a photograph with Paul.*

*An attractive Italian family: Paul, Jr. and his wife, Angela, on the occasion of the christening of their son, Paul Giuseppe Manno.*

*Mr. and Mrs. Manno have the chance to meet with Sopranos star "Medo," Jamie Lynn Sigler.*

# Pietro's

*A neighborhood institution, at the helm of Pietro's is John Iovaldi, Jr. and his son, John.*

After almost fifty years in business at the corner of Mardel and Watson, Pietro's must be doing something right. Three good reasons for their continued success include a good *cucina* (kitchen) at good value, old world charm, and last, but definitely not least, owner John Iovaldi, Jr., the son of one of Pietro's original founders, John Iovaldi, Sr., who in turn started the restaurant with Marco Griffero, Sr. When it comes to restaurant hospitality, John, Jr. is a king among princes.

During a crowded Friday lunch hour, John "in Cheers-like fashion" really does know everybody's name and what is current in their job and life. He greets not the Rat Pack but the Potato Pen pack, the gin players that used to meet for games downstairs for the past 15 years. At a neighboring table for ten, the conversation soundbites include which priests received an invitation to the Cardinals' spring training camp in Jupiter, Florida, and whether or not Stan Musial should be considered for canonization (Stan "the Man" lived a few doors down the street, off the alley on Mardel. Thus, his sainthood has already been long-accepted at the local level).

Among the faithful patrons is former Pietro's waiter, Mickey Garagiola. Known as the "Don Rickles" of the Hill's waiter community for good-naturedly insulting his customers, the now-retired Mickey is not only Joe's brother, but also an unofficial ambassador for the Hill. Having worked for Pietro's for decades, Mickey knows of the important place the restaurant has in the South St. Louis community. "For many years," he reminisces, "in South St Louis, Pietro's was the after-the-funeral restaurant. This was the drill: church, cemetery, Pietro's. And Marco Griffero's mother, Maria, was usually present, saying the rosary at the funeral (a tradition continued by her daughter, Gloria).

This corner meeting place and neighborhood institution started back in 1960 when John Iovaldi, Sr. and Marco Griffero picked the name "Pietro," Marco's middle name, for the restaurant (not to be confused with Del Pietros, which is a family named restaurant). The location they settled on was the former Charles Mittino's Supper Club. Marco had served as a busboy at Oldani's, Sala's, and Cafferata's in the 1940s, and he and John were co-workers at Magic Chef when they decided to strike out on their own as partners. After a brief stint as owners of Waldemar's Tavern off Manchester in Dogtown, they opened Pietro's. "It was a community-wide and family effort," John, Jr. explains. "All the aunts served as floor waitresses. An opening night waiter, Chick Severino, made $2 in tips and thought that was good!" The partners expanded to a second dining room in 1966 and a third in 1980.

Tragically, John, Sr. died on the day of John, Jr.'s graduation from St. Louis University High School. In the emergency situation, it was not long before the very young John, Jr. and Marco Griffero, Jr. took control of the management of their respective fathers' business. After many good years running the restaurant together, Marco, Jr. sold his interest to John, Jr. in 2004.

John, Jr. is happy to continue running the business co-founded by his father. Born and raised at the corner of Macklind and Wilson, and descended from a Northern Italian family, there is no other place for John Iovaldi than the Hill.

Besides longevity of staff, John is proud of the acquisition of Ruggeri chef Sebastian Murabito, who introduced his famous spinach balls and sauce to Pietro's. Of equal distinction is Pietro's signature sweet and tangy salad dressing, created by Emmalou, a 35-year veteran employee. "However," John says with a smile, "locals liked it better when we sold the salad dressing in the old whiskey bottles. It was those last few drops of alcohol dregs that they really latched onto."

Pietro's currently seats 275 people. "With the last expansion," says John, "I thought for sure we would find Al Capone's safe or buried cash. However, our treasure is in our employees and our customers."

To please the latter, John never changes the menu. "We have stayed true to our food and our menu." He displays on the wall a 1967 menu with many of the same items. Only the prices have changed. In 1967, an anchovy pizza cost $1.00, filet mignon $2.00, and lobster tail $4.00. "I remember we served two rock lobster tails per plate and customers often only would eat one. At the end of the night we busboys would gather up 20 untouched tails and feast, still throwing out half a dozen lobster tails!"

An oldie but goodie, Pietro's incorporates what is best in the spirit of a true Italian neighborhood eatery; love and respect for tradition, loyalty to employee and patron, and undeniable neighborhood pride.

155

John and Marianne were married in 1980 at St. Ambrose Church. Photo Below: The new patio, added in the summer of 2008, seats 50 people.

# BREAST OF CHICKEN MARIA

## INGREDIENTS

2 cups chicken stock

¼ tsp. garlic powder

1 tsp. lemon juice

1/3 cup sherry wine

½ cup (1 stick) butter

¼ cup flour

1½ cups (6 oz.) shredded Provel cheese

½ tsp. cracked black pepper

2 cups sliced fresh mushrooms

1 cup lump crabmeat

4 (6 oz. each) skinless and boneless chicken breasts

Additional flour

Extra-virgin olive oil

12 asparagus spears

## SAUCE

Bring chicken stock, garlic powder, lemon juice, and sherry to boil. In second pan, melt butter. Add flour, stirring constantly, until it is well absorbed and can be used as a roux for thickening; do not allow it to burn. Add roux to boiling ingredients, stirring constantly, until smooth. Reduce heat to low. Add Provel, black pepper, mushrooms, and crab meat. Heat thoroughly.

## CHICKEN AND ASPARAGUS

Salt and pepper chicken breasts and dredge in flour. Cook in a little hot oil until lightly browned on both sides. Cook asparagus separately.

## TO SERVE

Lay chicken pieces on platter. Place three asparagus spears on each breast. Ladle sauce over top of each serving.

SERVES 4

# SOLE SEBASTIAN

INGREDIENTS

*3 tbsp. butter*

*3 tbsp. flour*

*8 oz. cream*

*½ cup (2 oz.) grated Parmesan cheese*

*8 oz. lump crab meat*

*8 oz. cooked and peeled shrimp*

*8 oz. mushrooms, sliced*

*½ tsp. chopped garlic*

*1/3 cup white wine*

*1 tsp. lemon juice*

*Salt and pepper to taste*

*4 (6 oz. each) sole fillets*

*Additional flour*

*Extra-virgin olive oil*

*Chopped fresh parsley for garnish*

In skillet, melt butter. Whisk in flour, stirring constantly, until well absorbed; do not allow to burn. Gradually whisk in cream, heating until mixture thickens. Stir in Parmesan cheese. Keep cream sauce at simmer. Add crab meat, shrimp, mushrooms, garlic, wine, lemon juice, salt and pepper.

Season sole with salt and pepper. Dredge in flour. Heat small amount of olive oil in skillet. Cook sole until browned on both sides.

Place sole on platter and ladle sauce on top. Sprinkle with chopped parsley.

SERVES 4

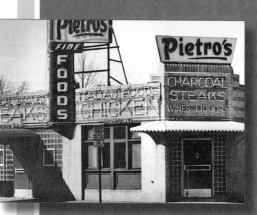

*Pietro's has gone through several changes over the years. This early view will be remembered by many.*

*Four Iovaldi aunts: Lena, Joanne, Rose, and Mary, worked at the restaurant.*

*The Iovaldi kids, left to right,: John Jr., Dan, Tim, Stephanie, and Nick pose for a Christmas card photo in 1998.*

159

# Portabella

Angela Del Pietro Zoog relates the story of how the name of their family restaurant came to be. "Thom and I were happily ensconced in Arizona, where he served as executive chef at the 5-Diamond Marquesa Fairmont Princess in Scottsdale and I was the Beverage Manager at the Hyatt Regency Scottsdale. In 1994, we received a call that my mother, Mary Rose Del Pietro, had become ill. I immediately returned home to help out at Del Pietro's Restaurant. While she recovered, my brother, Michael, went to look at the space formerly home to Port St. Louis. Sight unseen, my husband signed to launch our Clayton restaurant along with my brothers and cousins. To kick-start our new eatery, we held a 'Name the Restaurant' contest at Taste of Clayton. 'Portabella' was the winning entry. As we look back, we realized all this happened in the span of four months!"

The significant partnering of this couple seemed destined to be. After graduating from Nerinx Hall in Webster Groves, as did her mother be-fore her, Angela Del Pietro attended Arizona State in Tempe. While she worked as manager at the Sandolo Restaurant in Scottsdale, Thom Zoog was also on board as executive chef. Articulate and handsome, this former Boy Scout caught Angela's eye.

Raised in a small town in Ohio by Swiss-German parents, Thom Zoog learned how to forage for wild greens and berries under the tutelage of his Scoutmaster father. From his mother, he learned how to prepare homegrown vegetables. Today, his education is ongoing as he works with Beaver and Claverack Farms here in St. Louis to learn how to enhance dishes with honeysuckle and dandelion, a unique offering in Portabella's cutting-edge menu.

Presently, Thom works with Andy Ayers, former owner of Riddles Cafe, who connects restaurateurs with local farms. They work with "heirloom" vegetables—seeds over 100 years old—that produce the most flavorful produce. "When you graft and genetically change produce in order to turn out the most uniform-looking zucchini or kiwi, flavor is sacrificed," this well-versed chef comments.

If asked to describe their menu, Angela and Thom would say, "Tradition with a twist" as in toasted ravioli with goat cheese and tiramisu nestled in a phyllo shell. From day one, Portabella was famous for its delectable chicken ravioli and spinach, not to mention porcini mushroom risotto. To complement the menu, they offer an outstanding list of 350 wines from around the world

*The gracious Zoog family runs Portabella. Clockwise from top: Isabella, Executive Chef Thom, Angela Del Pietro Zoog, and Olivia.*

to delight the discerning palate. As an added touch, diners can view a portion of the 4,000-bottle inventory through a unique glass floor overlooking the cellar.

Both Angela and Thom have learned to please through the taste buds as well as through the force of their amiable personalities. Moving smoothly from one table to another, every patron is left with a contented smile upon their faces.

In the tough, competitive, and capricious world of food, the couple attest that the secret to their success is "Flexibility." Angela's great-grandmother, Mary Faille Palazzola, knew this when she initiated the restaurant heritage in 1926, along with grandmother Lee Russo, who started Rossino's, Saro's, and Pucci's locally and mother, Mary Rose Del Pietro, who established Del Pietro's and Michael's: they all would be proud of the Zoog's ongoing success.

As for Thom, he was able to come full circle from his boyhood days foraging for wild berries with his father and watching his favorite chefs on public TV. Dreaming that someday he would join the ranks and cook in front of an audience of millions, he was featured on Food Finds on the Food Network. To some that would seem a far cry from his days as a Boy Scout, but to Thom, a graduate from the Culinary Institute of America, who has worked for acclaimed chefs in New York, Dallas, Kansas City, and Phoenix, it was more of a natural progression and, to him, a coming home.

# CRISPY SCALLOPS

INGREDIENTS

1 shallot, slivered

1 cup dry white wine (pinot grigio)

3 whole black peppercorns

¼ cup lemon juice

1 tbsp. cream

1 cup (2 sticks) unsalted butter, cubed

Salt and pepper

4 whole sun-dried tomatoes,
    cut in julienne strips

8 basil leaves

Extra-virgin olive oil

12 jumbo scallops (10 per pound)

1 pkg. (1 lb.) frozen shredded
    phyllo dough (kataifi)

2 cloves garlic, chopped

12 oz. fresh spinach

### TOMATO-BASIL BEURRE BLANC

Combine shallot, white wine, peppercorns, and lemon juice in a non-reactive saucepan over high heat. Heat until reduced to 2 tablespoons liquid. Add cream. When liquid bubbles, reduce heat to low. Add butter, one cube at a time, whisking first on the heat and then off the heat. Continue whisking until mixture is fully combined to rich sauce consistency. Season with salt and pepper. Strain and discard shallots and peppercorn. Return sauce to pot. Stir in half the basil and sun-dried tomato.

### SCALLOPS

Season scallops with salt and pepper. Wrap with shredded phyllo dough. Heat skillet over medium-high heat and coat bottom with oil. Sear 1 side of each scallop about 3 minutes until golden brown. Place skillet in 400-degree oven for another 3 to 5 minutes until scallops are done.

### SPINACH

Heat large skillet and coat bottom with extra-virgin olive oil. Saute remaining garlic and sun-dried tomato 2 to 3 minutes. Add spinach. Toss. Cook until wilted. Season with salt and pepper.

### ASSEMBLY

Place one-fourth of spinach on center of each plate. Top with 3 scallops. Drizzle and circle plate with tomato-basil beurre blanc. Serve immediately.

SERVES 4

*Guests are delighted with a walk over the glass ceiling above the 4,000-bottle wine cellar.*

*Before tying the knot, the young couple dated in Arizona while Thom served as executive chef in a Five-Diamond restaurant.*

*Thom enjoys a special moment with his two daughters, Isabella and, at right, Olivia.*

# EGGPLANT TOWER

### INGREDIENTS

Extra-virgin olive oil

1 small onion, chopped

1 head garlic

1 eggplant, cut in eight (½-inch-thick) circles, drained on paper towels

1 bunch Swiss chard

2 tomatoes, chopped

½ cup water

Salt and pepper

4 small portobello mushrooms, stems removed

4 large basil leaves, cut chiffonade

Balsamic vinegar

2 eggs

1 cup milk

2 cups dried breadcrumbs

Flour for dredging

2 balls fresh Mozzarella cheese, cut in eight (¼-inch-thick) slices

2 cups marinara sauce

### SWISS CHARD

Coat heavy-bottom pot with extra-virgin olive oil. Cook onion and 2 to 4 cloves garlic until moist. Add Swiss chard, tomato, and water. Season with salt and pepper. Stew about 20 minutes until tender.

### PORTOBELLO MUSHROOMS

Rub mushrooms with extra-virgin olive oil. Sprinkle on 4-6 cloves minced garlic, basil, salt, and pepper. Broil or grill about 5 minutes per side, depending on size, until tender. Remove from broiler or grill and drizzle hot mushrooms with balsamic vinegar. Set aside.

### EGGPLANT

Dredge eggplant in flour. Submerge in egg wash, formed by mixing eggs and milk, then coat with crumbs. In skillet, heat thin layer of extra-virgin olive oil. Cook eggplant until golden brown on both sides with soft interior. Drain on paper towels.

### ASSEMBLE TOWER

Preheat oven to 400 degrees. Lay 4 pieces of eggplant on baking sheet. Top each with 2 slices of cheese. Broil 5 minutes to melt the cheese. Top each with one-fourth of Swiss chard, 1 mushroom and remaining eggplant. Heat in oven for 10 minutes or until tower is hot throughout. Serve immediately on plate with warm marinara sauce.

Hint: To cut basil chiffonade, roll leaves tightly into cigar shape, then slice across the roll into thin strips.

### SERVES 4

# Rich & Charlie's

When it comes to discussing terms or sealing the deal on their many franchise operations, Rich & Charlie's has a no-fail method: take two hands, clasp together and shake—making it a done deal. When it comes to discussing profit sharing, it's, "Oh, hmm, by the way…" and that's the end of the discussion. Next, they'll change the subject by saying, "Now get back to work and produce the best-tasting Italian food the whole family can enjoy at a reasonable price."

Way back when, St. Louis' Italian dining scene was pretty predictable. Every menu listed lasagna and spaghetti and meatballs as their main entrées. Then, along came Richard Ronzio and Charlie Mugavero who initiated a ground breaking era by including many of the popular dishes St. Louis enjoys today. After meeting at Andreino's (later Dominic's) on the Hill, the two paired up and opened an Italian/Jewish Deli in University City. Along with the cannelloni and cavatelli, they also served knishes, pastrami on rye, and sweet and sour cabbage. Oi vey, mamma mia.

St. Louis cried out for an encore, so they opened a second location—a carry out restaurant on the corner of Woods Mill and Clayton roads. Needing to add something dynamic to their repertoire, the ambitious duo of Rich and Charlie, now teamed up with John Ferrara, to establish a fine dining trattoria near Forest Park. With a handshake and a pat on the back, Rich and Charlie franchised the Lemay Ferry location to their nephews, Marty Ronzio and Emil Pozzo in 1973, which Marty still oper-

*Left to right: Emil Pozzo, Emil Pozzo (Father), Chuck R. Pozzo, Paul Ronzio, Martin Ronzio, Joe Puleo, and Chuck Pozzo constitute the affable Rich & Charlie's team.*

ates today. Emil currently manages the Rich & Charlie's on Watson Road along with his son, Emil, and Marty Ronzio's son, Paul.

Also taking advantage of the franchise opportunity was Emil's brother, Chuck, and his brother-in-law, Dominic Puleo, when the two took over the Woods Mill and Clayton site in 1973. Two years later, Chuck built a Rich & Charlie's across the Missouri River, which is currently operating in St. Peters. Business grew even further when a few of Rich and Charlie's friends and business associates, Kim Tucci and Joe Fresta, opened a franchise in Ballwin on Manchester Road in 1974. The franchises multiplied like bunnies, and each one became

a great success. Could it be the quality of the food, the friendliness of the staff and management or is it the family-friendly pricing? Marty Ronzio acknowledges that it is all three of the above. Each franchise owner follows in the footsteps of the original Rich & Charlie's, established in 1967, which was founded on the simple philosophy of "taking the whole family out for a delicious Italian dinner at a great American price."

Suddenly, seven years after opening the door of the first Rich & Charlie's, one half of the dynamic duo, Charlie Mugavero, and his wife were killed in a plane crash while flying to Mexico for a belated honeymoon. Reformulating after the tragedy, the franchise team of Rich Ronzio, Marty Ronzio, Emil Pozzo, Kim Tucci, John Ferrara, and Joe Fresta began the Pasta House Co. concept of restaurants. Later, the group bought Rich's share in 1979. At that time, the company included twelve Rich & Charlie's/Pasta House Co. locations, including one in Kansas City and one in the Galleria in Houston. In 1981, Emil and Marty decided to spin off the Pasta House Company to Tucci, Fresta, and Ferrarra.

Following in the footsteps of the original team is a new generation of franchise owners. Marty's son, Paul, and Emil's son, Chuck, joined together in 1997 to establish a Rich & Charlie's in Eureka. Today, there are five Rich & Charlie's locations in the St. Louis metropolitan area.

When Marty and Emil are prodded about the success and longevity of their 40-year partnership, Emil shares their secret, "Marty runs the Lemay location and I run the Watson restaurant. We are our own boss and don't tell each other what to do." Is that all? "We know how to cook, but we prefer to be greeting our customers." On a Saturday night, the Watson location serves 300-400 and Lemay will average 500-600.

As to who created the signature Rich & Charlie's salad, Marty is quick to offer, "Rich and Charlie are the ones who put together the iceberg and romaine lettuce, fresh-grated Parmesan, artichoke hearts, pimento, and red onions. The salad is still the same today." Some people ask about the strangeness of having linguine and chicken livers on the menu. "Maybe it was my uncle's Jewish enclave in University City that popularized this dish," says Marty. "Every six months, we talk about dropping it, but our customers just keep ordering it."

But, what the franchise owners enjoy the most is, "Seeing families and friends coming together, knowing they enjoy our version of the Italian table, without having to break the bank." No wonder the Rich & Charlie's "family" has been so successful!

*The Ronzio grandparents ran Ronzio Grocery on Sublette and Bischoff. The woman behind the counter, Guilina, stands next to her husband, Martino Ronzio. The little girl is Perina Ronzio.*

*An early photo of Emil and Perina Ronzio Pozzo in their backyard on Shaw and Macklind. Perina is the mother of current owners Emil and Chuck Pozzo.*

# RICH & CHARLIE'S SALAD

INGREDIENTS

*3 cups iceberg lettuce, chopped*

*1 cup romaine lettuce, chopped*

*½ cup artichoke hearts, preferably canned*

*¼ cup diced pimento*

*¼ cup sliced red onion*

*4 oz. freshly grated Parmesan cheese*

*3 oz. (3/8 cup) Rich & Charlie's salad dressing*

In large salad bowl, combine iceberg and romaine lettuce, artichoke, pimento, red onion, and cheese. Toss thoroughly with dressing.

RICH & CHARLIE'S SALAD DRESSING:

Combine 4 ounces (1/2 cup) red wine vinegar, 11 ounces (1-3/8 cups) vegetable oil, 1 ounce (2 tablespoons) olive oil, 1 teaspoon salt, and ½ teaspoon black pepper. Makes 2 cups dressing.

SERVES 4

Emil and Perina Ronzio Pozzo prepare homemade ravioli, a Christmas tradition.

# PASTA CON BROCCOLI

INGREDIENTS

1 lb. cavatelli pasta (small shells with rolled edges)

1 tbsp. salt

2 pints half-and-half cream

½ cup (1 stick) butter

1½ cups sliced fresh mushrooms

2 cups fresh broccoli, crowns only, blanched

¼ cup favorite marinara sauce

3 cloves garlic, finely chopped

Pinch red pepper

Pinch black pepper

¼ tsp. salt

6 oz. freshly grated Parmesan cheese

Bring large pot of water to boil. Add pasta and salt. Cook pasta al dente. Drain in a colander. Return pasta to pot along with half-and-half, butter, mushrooms, broccoli, marinara, garlic, red and black pepper and salt. Bring to boil, stirring occasionally, or until half-and-half starts to froth. Remove from heat. Stir in Parmesan cheese. Serve immediately. Mangia!

SERVES 4-6

Pictured, left to right, are Carol and Chuck Pozzo with Anne and Paul Ronzio at the opening night of the Eureka Rich & Charlie's in 1997.

In 1958, Paul Ronzio, father of Marty Ronzio, operated Roncaro's on Manchester Road in Rock Hill. He also owned one of the first area pizza parlors, Pagliacci's, during the 1950s, partnering with Bob Cassulo.

Rigazzi's

# *Tony's*

The legend began in 1946 when Tony Bommarito, Sr. opened Tony's Spaghetti House. Upon his father's untimely death in 1949, son Vincent, just 18, stepped up with his brother, Tony Jr., to operate his family's restaurant. Vince vowed that one day he would run one of the finest restaurants. As we all know, Vince realized his dream and then some.

Tony's has a long pedigree, steeped in both St. Louis' rich history and its culinary lore. On Vince's mother (Lucille's) side, the Randazzos owned the Randazzo Macaroni Company at the intersection of 10th and Carr streets in downtown St. Louis. On his father's side, the Bommaritos operated the city's first Italian bakery at the intersection of 7th and Carr streets in the 1890s. In 1934, Vince's father opened the New Deal Restaurant at the intersection of Hadley Street and Franklin Avenue, which is now the site of the America's Center Convention Complex. It closed during the Depression, but the Spaghetti House at the intersection of Broadway and Franklin Avenue followed and the rest, they say, is history.

Being an innovator, Vince transitioned the Spaghetti House to Tony's Spaghetti and Steak House. Tony, Jr. and Vince displayed prime cuts of steak in their display case in the window in order to tempt passersby. Soon, the business doubled in size. Hopeful restaurateurs knew then to work and study under Vince to learn his methodology. A St. Louis family of successful restaurateurs descended from Tony's, including Dominic Galati, Kim Tucci, Paul

*The Bommarito family which, over the years, has garnered numerous distinguished awards is, left to right, Vince, Jr., Anthony, Vince, and James.*

Manno, John Mineo, and Giovanni Gabriele.

An unforgettable experience, patrons always remember when Tony's staff used to walk backwards to guide them up the elegant staircase to the dining area, never turning their back on a guest.

Today, St. Louisans proudly claim Tony's, and its many awards, as their own. The honors continue to multiply: the Mobil 5 Star Award, the Condé Nast Best Italian Restaurant Award, and a Restaurant News Hall of Fame recipient. As typical of Vince, all of these recognitions are tucked away in the office and not on display in the restaurant.

While it might seem that fine dining in St. Louis cannot get any better, Vince is still at the restaurant six days a week because he understands that Tony's is only as good as each and

every meal, each and every evening.

Vince insists that his customers are the "pulse of the place." But, in order for them to experience the best he has to offer, he taught his staff an orderly, innovative, and precise system that helps to reduce stress and encourage a "hospitality frame of mind." Even communication amongst the kitchen staff is regulated so it never increases above a certain volume. Moreover, as early as the 1950s, Vince and Tony made sure the kitchen was air-conditioned.

Procedurally, there is never any question as to what will happen next even when the staff hosts as many as 200 diners on a typical Saturday night. (His system worked so well that many of his employees stayed for 30 to 40 years.)

Updating the décor to provide an elegant

backdrop, keeping index cards on customers, introducing table side dinner service, and fine-tuning the menus to include vegetarian entrees and other specific dietary requests keeps Tony's on the cutting-edge of the industry.

It is Vince's driving "hospitality mentality" that has enabled all of St. Louis to benefit from Vince's love of the town. It comes as no surprise that he has put his considerable talents to work on behalf of St. Louis. Vince credits his continued success to the support and encouragement of his beloved wife, Martha. While she stood by his side for 50 years, he has garnered such acclaim as an entrant into the National and Missouri Hall of Fame as well as receiving the Man of the Year award from the Italian American Organization and the Dr. Martin Luther King, Jr. Community Award. Vince has been honored on both sides of the Atlantic as the

Italian Government inducted him into the Order of the Cavaliers and the Sons of the Revolution, presenting him with the Modern Patriot Award. His civic involvement covers a broad canvas including groups such as Operation Brightside, the St. Louis Community College Foundation, March of Dimes Auction, and the Boys' Club of St. Louis. Currently a Commissioner for the St. Louis City Police, Vince holds leadership positions in several organizations dedicated to the growth and beautification of St. Louis' downtown area.

The "restaurant gene" has now passed down to his sons, James, Vince, Jr., and Anthony, and his daughter, Lucy Ann. Youngest daughter, Diana, originally worked in the hospitality industry for Maritz Travel. In particular, Vince, Jr. always knew he wanted to one day contribute to this restaurant dynasty. He attended the Culinary

Institute of America and, like his father before him, is hands-on when it comes to supervising the kitchen, preparing special sauces, and then donning his brightest smile when he goes out front to greet the guests.

Many years have passed and Vince, C.E.O. of Tony's, is still taking care of business. It shows in his dedication, his masterful innovations, and his fierce loyalty to staff and clientele. As a result, Tony's continues to receive numerous accolades from internationally known restaurant associations, travel magazines, and business clubs.

At the end of the day, what Vince understands is that to be successful, you have to like people. Everyone looks for him in the dining room because they know that he is genuinely happy to see them. Tony's has become synonymous with St. Louis, and Vince Bommarito is the quintessential ambassador.

# HONEY-GLAZED FIGS
## WITH GORGONZOLA

INGREDIENTS

10 figs

1 cup honey

1 cup white wine

1 tbsp. dried lavender

1 cinnamon stick

Gorgonzola cheese

In a small sauce pan, bring honey, white wine, cinnamon, and lavender to a simmer. Add figs, one by one, to the pan. Poach the figs for 2-3 minutes. Figs should still be firm. Remove the figs with a slotted spoon. Reduce liquid by half and strain out lavender and cinnamon stick.

Cut the figs in half, crosswise. Place bottoms on oven-proof pan and put a small piece of Gorgonzola cheese on the fig, then place under broiler to melt the cheese slightly. Replace the tops of the figs. Divide figs onto five plates, drizzle with the honey sauce. Serve with warm bread as a cheese/fruit course.

SERVES 5

*Above: Tony's Spaghetti & Steak House at the intersection of Broadway and Franklin Avenue was expanded and remodeled several times. Center Top Photo: To ensure the high quality they've become known for, Vince and his brother, Tony, Jr., cut their own steaks and meat products.*

*Above: A clamoring, hungry crowd at Tony's Spaghetti & Steak House. Tony tends bar while Vince speaks with the customers.*

*Left: Vince has great pride in his kitchen operation where order, efficiency, productivity, and cleanliness are held to the highest standard in the industry.*

180

# SEARED SCALLOPS WITH BLACK TRUFFLES

INGREDIENTS

*1 cup white wine*

*1 cup heavy cream*

*¼ lb. butter*

*Salt and white pepper to taste*

*½ teaspoon black truffles*

*10 sea scallops, large*

*Olive oil*

Combine wine and cream in a small sauce pan and reduce by half. Whip in ¼ pound butter, season with salt, white pepper, and truffles. Set aside in a warm place.

Season scallops with salt and pepper. Heat olive oil in shallow pan. Sear scallops on both sides until lightly brown. Divide scallops onto five plates. Spoon the truffle butter over scallops and serve.

SERVES 5

*Vince, at left, and Tony, at right, accept one of their numerous awards from the March of Dimes organization.*

*In the beginning, Tony's was famous for their homemade pies. Vince is pictured with, left to right, his sister, Joan (Bommarito) Campo; his godmother, Marie Schulte; his mother, Lucille; and his grandmother, Mrs. Randazzo.*

*In 1963, young Anthony has the opportunity to meet the legendary Stan Musial during the last year he played Major League baseball.*

# Trattoria Marcella

Who ever knew a moment of child rebellion could lead to gourmet greatness? Yet, Steve and Jamie Komorek have proven that sometimes father and mother do not always know best, that sometimes a child, or children in this case, must follow the call of their hearts.

Steve and Jamie heard the call while driving home from Las Vegas in 1990. While in the vicinity of the Hoover Dam, the brothers turned to each other and said, "Let's start up our own restaurant!"

Though it was not as if a life in the restaurant business was truly out of the main for the exuberant brothers who descended from a long line of St. Louis restaurateurs, the Slay family. Indeed, the brothers' grandfather opened the first Slay family-owned restaurant in downtown St. Louis almost a century ago in 1911. That first restaurant was followed by the opening of multiple Slay-owned eateries in the St. Louis metropolitan area over the next 80 to 90 years.

Nevertheless, the brothers' father, James Komorek, and mother, Marcella Slay Komorek, always warned them not to go into the restaurant business because it was a time-consuming life. Yet, it was hard for the brothers, who are cousins to current Mayor Francis Slay, to avoid the restaurant scene. For starters, they grew up in the incredible culinary milieu of the Hill. Their senses took in the delicious aromas every time they walked to school at St. Ambrose, where Steve went to grade school, although the

*The Komorek siblings, Steve, Christine, and Jamie, stand in front of their outstanding wine cellar.*

brothers grew up in St. Louis Hills. Then, as they grew into adolescence, the need for pocket money and family history drew them to the restaurants for employment. "My first job was a busboy when I was 12 at Bartolino's," Jamie recalls. "Then in my late teens I worked for seven years for David Slay restaurants." When he waited tables at Mike Shannon's in 1985, he met his Sicilian-born wife, Patricia, who served as hostess.

Consequently, despite parental warnings, the brothers had restaurants in their blood. Within a few years of their Hoover Dam epiphany, Trattoria Marcella, named for their late mother, was born.

"We decided we would make a fun, vibrant, relaxed restaurant—not high end, but a place we would want to dine in ourselves," says Jamie. Being young twenty-somethings and strapped for cash, they looked for a site at bargain basement rates and found one on the

corner of Pernod and Watson, formerly home to a ravioli factory and Ron & Shirley's Pizzeria. Four years later, the first round of expansion changed the seating from 60 to 100. "We got tired of telling people they had to wait two weeks to dine here," they remarked. A second remodeling increased seating to 150, but, unfortunately, knocked out the brothers' herb, tomato, and arugula garden out back.

As for the cuisine, Steve laughingly reminisces, "In our teens, we figured if we knew how to make a lemon butter and cream sauce we knew all there was to opening an Italian trattoria."

Since those early days, Steve and Jamie have moved light years beyond cream sauce, creating an extraordinary restaurant with exquisite food that has been named by *Gourmet Magazine* as one of America's Top Ten Tables in the 24 cities reviewed by the prestigious magazine.

Jamie is the general manager of the operation, managing the wait staff and the wine inventory, while Steve currently serves as the restaurant's executive chef. For Trattoria Marcella, the brothers have developed a rich menu that they term, "Piedmont to Palermo," in that it reflects culinary styles from all parts of Italy. In particular, the menu highlights risotto. Over the years of honing his craft, Steve has learned the subtlety of risotto, understanding that it requires time, care, and even a knowledge of the moisture content in the air to know what amount of chicken stock is perfect for that particular day. The result of this culinary journey is risotto perfection that for years has drawn a host of diners, especially many of Northern Italian persuasion.

The menu also reveals a deep respect for Italian culinary history. For example, aspects of the restaurant's Sicilian-based dishes, such as artichoke stuffed with couscous and the use of toasted pine nuts, exemplify in food the influence of Sicily's Greek, Spanish, and North-African conquerors.

This respect for history has led Steve to become involved with Slow Food, a non-profit, eco-gastronomic international organization that was founded in Italy in 1989. Steve explains enthusiastically that the mission of Slow Food is "to counteract fast food and fast life, to prevent the disappearance of local food traditions, and how our food choices affect the rest of the world. For example, there once were 14 different breeds of pigs, some sweet, some briny. Because of diners' dwindling interest in the food they eat, that count fell down to two. Now thanks to the Slow Food organization the original 14 breeds have been restored."

Steve spent 14 weeks in Eastern Italy learning about regional olives, *salumi* (salami), and wine. He visited farm fields, vineyards, factories, and wineries and returned home full of excitement and culinary ideas. Many of these delicious concepts found their way onto the menu of Trattoria Marcella.

The success of Trattoria Marcella proves that sometimes a little rebellion is necessary for greatness. Not only is this restaurant a true family affair–their sister, Christine, works alongside her brothers, managing catering–it is a culinary jewel in St. Louis.

# POLENTA FRIES
## WITH CARAMELIZED MARSALA
## GORGONZOLA CREAM SAUCE

### INGREDIENTS
3 cups chicken stock (or broth
    or water)
3 cups heavy whipping cream
½ tsp. salt
1 box (13.2 oz.) instant polenta
¼ cup grated Parmesan cheese
oil for frying

### SAUCE
750 ml. bottle of Marsala wine
1 pint heavy whipping cream
½ tsp. minced garlic
small sprig of fresh rosemary
1 tsp. sugar
½ cup (2 oz.) imported Gorgonzola
    cheese, crumbled
3 tbsp. sweet butter
4 cups assorted mushrooms, sliced
    and roasted

*Above: Jamie walks among the vines in Valpolicella in Italy. Below: A special alcove in the restaurant honors Jamie and Steve's mother, Marcella.*

### POLENTA FRIES

Combine chicken stock, 3 cups cream, and salt in a sauce pan. Bring to boil. Add polenta. Cook and stir, using a wooden spoon, until polenta pulls away from pot. Add Parmesan. Spread mixture on baking sheet until evenly ¼-inch thick. Chill.

Preheat oil to 350 degrees. Slice polenta into sticks to desired width to resemble fries. Fry sticks in oil until golden brown and crisp. Remove fries from oil. Drain on paper towels.

### MARSALA GORGONZOLA SAUCE AND MUSHROOMS

Heat Marsala wine until reduced to syrupy consistency. In separate sauce pan, cook 1 pint cream until reduced by half. Combine both mixtures in single skillet. Add garlic, rosemary, sugar, and cheese. Cook 4 to 5 minutes over medium heat until cheese melts. Add butter and mushrooms. Cook until mushrooms are just done and butter is well incorporated.

Serve fries with favorite marinara sauce or Marsala Gorgonzola cream sauce and sautéed mushrooms, listed above.

SERVES 4-6

*Jamie enjoys lunch in the mountains of Ravello, high above the Amalfi Coast.*

# LOBSTER RISOTTO

### INGREDIENTS

| | |
|---|---|
| *2 tsp. extra-virgin olive oil* | *4½ cups lobster stock (or clam juice* |
| *½ small onion, diced* | *diluted with water), kept hot* |
| *2 ½ tbsp. butter* | *½ cup tomato sauce* |
| *½ cup sliced assorted mushrooms* | *5 oz. cooked lobster meat* |
| *½ tsp. chopped garlic* | *1 cup fresh spinach* |
| *½ cup dry white wine* | *½ cup grated Parmigiano* |
| *1 cup uncooked Arborio rice* | *Reggiano cheese* |
| | *Salt and white pepper to taste* |

In medium pot with 4-inch side, heat oil. Lightly cook onion, stirring often, until translucent. Add butter and mushrooms. Cook, stirring often, until mushrooms are soft. Add garlic. Cook quickly, while stirring, until slightly toasted. Add wine and cook until mixture is reduced by half. Add Arborio rice, 1 cup stock, and tomato sauce. Over low heat, continue to cook and stir, adding stock as needed, until rice has desired bite and texture. When the stock is completely absorbed, add lobster, spinach, and Parmigiano Reggiano cheese at one time. Mix all ingredients. Season with salt and pepper.

SERVES 4 AS STARTER COURSE

## Slay's Bar Barbecue
### A la Carte Dinner

Includes - Salad, French Fries, Bread and Butter
Mushrooms and Gravy 35c Extra

| | |
|---|---|
| BAR-B-Q CHICKEN | 1.60 |
| 1-2 FRIED CHICKEN | 1.50 |
| FILET MIGNON | 2.50 |
| STRIP STEAK | 2.75 |
| T-BONE STEAK | 1.95 |
| SPECIAL (2) BAR-B-Q PORK CHOPS | 1.95 |
| PORK | 1.00 |
| BEEF | 1.00 |
| HAMBURGER STEAK, Grilled Onion Rings | 1.00 |
| LIVER & GIZZARDS | 1.00 |
| JACK SALMON, Tartar Sauce | 1.00 |
| CHANNEL CAT FISH, Saute | 1.25 |
| FRENCH FRIED SHRIMP, Cocktail Sauce | 1.00 |

*The Komorek brothers were inspired by their mother, Marcella Slay, and the Slay family of restaurants.*

*The Komorek brothers participate in the biennial Taste of Tilles fund raiser.*

# Yacovelli's

*The current owners of this four-generation restaurant are Jack and Jan Yacovelli.*

There are few people who have lived a significant part of their lives in the St. Louis area who have not heard of Yacovelli's, or at least of Mr. Yac's as some in North St. Louis County used to know it. Over the past 90 years, the restaurant has been situated in nine different locations around the St. Louis metropolitan area. From these various locations, Yacovelli's has served residents of the City of St. Louis, South and North County patrons, and Washington University students. Probably tens of thousands of St. Louisans have entered Yacovelli's doors for a wedding, high school reunion, or club meeting. Like toasted raviolis and gooey butter cake, Yacovelli's is a place true St. Louisans know.

The tradition began when John and Filomena ("Fanny") Yacovelli left their home in the Italian province of Campania, located between Rome and Naples. Crossing the Atlantic on the *Dewey*, Mr. and Mrs. Yacovelli and their newborn son arrived in America in the early part of the 20th Century. As the family story goes, the two eventually settled in St. Louis, where John found a restaurant job working for a count who ran up a terrible tab with his love of wine. John offered to pay the count's wine bill, if the count agreed to give his restaurant to John. The count, wishing to be free of the burden, immediately agreed, thereby making John and Fanny the owners of a restaurant at the corner of Vandeventer and Laclede. The year was 1919.

From that point onward, the restaurant moved several times, with their mid-century location at Millbrook and Big Bend being one of the most popular, as the dedicated students of Washington University loved the Italian eatery, especially during finals week, when the strong black coffee served got many a Wash U. student through an all-nighter. To this day Wash U. alum still have a soft spot in their hearts for Yacovelli's, as evidenced by the fact that more than one Wash U. reunion has been celebrated there.

By 1950, John and Fanny's son, Dewey (named for the ship that brought the family to America), had taken over the business. In that year he and his wife, Marie, moved the restaurant to Kirkwood in the area of Big Bend and Highway 44. It was at this location where Dewey changed restaurant history by inventing the salad bar.

Previously, customers always had to wait for their entrees without anything to satisfy their hunger. Dewey saw a need to fill in this interim and envisioned a buffet which would keep customers happy until the main course was served. However, Dewey knew that if the salad bar was going to work he would need a huge bowl in which to hold the salad offerings. Finding such a massive bowl proved difficult. As Jack, Dewey's son, remembers, "We almost used the cone of a B-52 bomber! But then a smaller replica became available from a friend who was making a concave observation porthole for the St. Louis Zoo Aquarium."

With that porthole Dewey changed restaurants forever, starting a trend that would spread nationwide and which is still thriving today.

However, in 1957, Marie became very ill, thereby necessitating the sale of the restaurant until such time as she recovered. As part of the sale Dewey agreed that when Marie returned to health he would not open up a competing restaurant within a 15-mile radius of the Kirkwood location. Hence the 1967 christening of Yacovelli's in North St. Louis County on Dunn Road.

During the years of Dewey's tenure, he mentored his son, Jack, in the ways of the restaurant business. Even as far back as the age of four, Jack remembers standing on an orange crate, sorting silverware. By his teens, Jack had met the love of his life, Jan, who started as the coat-check girl at the age of 15. Jack and Jan married on July 18th, 1971, and by 1977, they had taken over management of the business, with Jack running the kitchen and Jan serving as front-end manager and interior decorator.

"Today I have the best job," Jan says enthusiastically, "helping brides plan the best day of their lives, for a Yacovelli wedding banquet."

The facility seats 450 people. As a result, according to Jack, "Half the people we meet have attended a special event at our facility."

A vibrant and highly personable couple, Jack and Jan Yacovelli were named 2007 Restaurateurs of the Year by the Missouri Restaurant Association. This award was well-deserved, not only because of Jack and Jan's warm welcome to patrons and the long history of the establishment, but also because the couple has remained true to the restaurant's commitment to offering excellent European-style cuisine.

The Yacovellis respect the wonderful dishes that have garnered the loyalty of patrons for decades. Indeed, Jack's grandmother, Fanny, though using a walker, still came into the restaurant until the age of 96 to prepare the homemade raviolis served by the restaurant. "From years of rolling out that dough," Jack says, "she was so strong that she could arm wrestle!"

But Jack, the man who grew up in the Yacovelli kitchen, has a passion for food inside of him, and he constantly experiments with recipes that will fit into the European flavor his patrons have come to expect.

Today, Jack and Jan are the mentors for five grandchildren who get up on milk crates and learn to make gnocchi or ravioli or whatever delicious item the culinary muse inspires their grandfather to create. Perhaps the next great Yacovelli restaurateur is standing on one of those crates.

# BRASCIOLE

### INGREDIENTS

*½ cup green onions*

*2 tbsp. garlic, fresh*

*½ cup olive oil (for Stuffing)*

*2 cups Italian breadcrumbs*

*1 cup Parmesan cheese*

*2 eggs*

*2 cups day-old French bread, cubed*

*1 round steak*

*Salt and pepper to taste*

*3 cups tomato sauce*

*If mixture is too dry, add milk*

Stuffing: Sauté green onions and garlic in olive oil. In a mixing bowl, add the olive oil mixture to breadcrumbs, Parmesan cheese, eggs, and cubed French bread. Mix well. If stuffing mixture is too dry, add milk.

Pound round steak with meat hammer until it's between ¼ to ½-inch thick. Season with salt and pepper. Add stuffing mixture and pat down to about ½-inch thickness.

Roll round steak and tie with string. Sauté the meat in olive oil until brown. Simmer in tomato sauce approximately 45 minutes.

SERVES 4

*Dewey Yacovelli outside his restaurant located at Sappington and Big Bend in Kirkwood.*

*Filomena and John Yacovelli enjoy a special time together.*

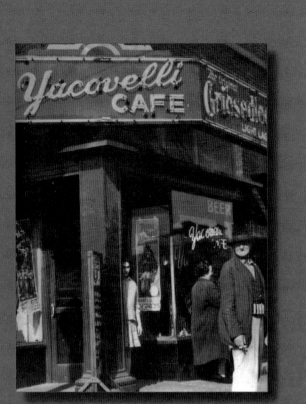

*The Grand and Park location was operated by John and his family for many years. This area would become part of Children's Hospital.*

*Jack's mother, Maria, serves from Yacovelli's famous salad bar.*

# PARMESAN-ENCRUSTED TILAPIA

### INGREDIENTS

*1 cup Italian breadcrumbs*

*1 cup Parmesan cheese*

*Four 7 oz. tilapia filets*

*½ white onion, chopped*

*½ tomato, fresh, chopped*

*¼ cup olive oil*

*1 tsp. leaf oregano*

*1 tsp. basil*

Breading mixture: Mix breadcrumbs and Parmesan cheese together.

Wet tilapia in water and dredge in breading mixture. Place in small baking dish and add water to cover bottom of dish. Bake uncovered for approximately 7 minutes at 450 degrees.

While fish is cooking, sauté onions and tomatoes in olive oil until onions are lightly browned, approximately 3-4 minutes. Add spices and simmer on low heat until fish is done. Pour over tilapia and serve.

SERVES 4

*Robyn and Dennis Chiodini with their daughter, Cory Chiodini-May.*

# Zia's

For many St. Louisans, the Hill represents a flourishing Italian neighborhood and great Italian food. To Dennis and Angelo Chiodini, who opened Zia's "On The Hill" in 1984, the Hill represents a fruitful family business that has seen success for three generations.

Born as second-generation citizens on the Hill, Dennis and his brother, Angelo, were raised by a close-knit family that found its roots in the city of Marcalo in the Italian province of Lombardy. In fact, their grandparents once owned one of the early Hill bakeries.

As was typical of Hill teenagers in the 1960s, Dennis bussed and waited tables and parked cars at old establishments like Andreino's and Rigazzi's. "We all worked the circuit," Dennis remembers. "It gets in your blood though, growing up into it and constantly surrounded by great cooks, recipes, and food."

Therefore, it was a natural step for Dennis and Angelo to open a restaurant, which they did at the corner of Wilson and Edwards

in May of 1984. This building once housed Consolino's Grocery, one of Dennis' former employers when he was a teenager. Dennis did a lot of the remodeling, transitioning it into a full-service restaurant. The front dining room was formerly the dry goods store and the kitchen had been the garage. Eventually, the old Consolino grocery warehouse was transformed into a 160-seat restaurant, capable of serving 700 dinners on a Saturday night.

Zia's "On the Hill" is named for two great cooks–the aunts of Dennis and Angelo ("zia" means "aunt" in Italian). "When we first opened," says Dennis, "Zia Anne oversaw the kitchen staff and made sure they were doing everything to her satisfaction. Zia Lena stood outside directing customers to 'Eat in,' pointing to the front door or 'Take out,' through our carry-out window." Edna Chiodini, Dennis' mother, lived in an apartment above the restaurant but made her daily appearance during lunch. There was a special table in the bar area where she sat everyday, visiting with local

customers and employees. Many Zia friends also remember Dennis' sister, Beverly, who worked in the office as well as helping with carry out until she retired. Last but not least, Paul Chiodini, brother of Zia Anne and Zia Lena, has been a faithful worker from day one. He lives one block from Zia's and has answered the call of duty for Dennis and Angelo, handling anything from tasting new recipes to opening the doors for suppliers. The only charge for his service was tiramisu—a prized family recipe—or a piece of double chocolate layer cake to take home.

The tradition of family contribution and involvement has passed on to the next generation. Angelo's son, Louie, also made his mark in the prep room when he was young while Angelo's wife, Gerry, spent time behind the scenes assisting with the bookkeeping. The Chiodini children also came up through the ranks: oldest son, Jason, progressed from busboy to line cook; while daughter, Michelle, seated guests; younger son, Nicholas, bussed tables alongside his sister, Cory, who waitressed and currently manages the restaurant. Her husband, Michael May, serves as comptroller and oversees the catering business.

Known for its moderately priced, generously portioned gourmet food and casual atmosphere, the success of Zia's is a result of the strong family commitment to make the restaurant a place that is warm and comfortable. Angelo Chiodini has since retired, while owners, Dennis and Robyn Chiodini, continue the strong family tradition of Zia's "On the Hill." Dennis' wife, Robyn, came from a strong, Italian family. She critiques new recipes, runs the Web site and online store for Zia's products. She is thrilled with the international popularity of Zia's Sweet Italian Salad Dressing, which has even been shipped to servicemen worldwide.

The Chiodinis are proud of their traditional, locally produced and family-centered cuisine. Italian wines, unique appetizers, and made-to-order daily specials which all offer the true taste of Italy. Zia's toasted ravioli is a customer favorite. In fact, Dennis received a call from a desperate Italian restaurant owner in California who said "St. Louis Cardinal, Mark McGwire, has retired here and he is driving me crazy for your toasted raviolis! Please, please, tell me how you make them!" Visitors from the gourmet strongholds of New York and Boston rave over Zia's garlic cream sauce. Perhaps the biggest selling appetizer is the fried calamari –calamari fritti. Zia's serves over 250 pounds of calamari fritti every week.

"Our famous round table in the bar," notes Robyn, "has been a popular gathering place for long-time customers to laugh and reminisce with our restaurant family. Yogi Berra often enjoys a meal at Zia's every time he returns home to visit his sister, Josie. She has shared a lot of the Yogi memorabilia we feature on our walls."

As the Chiodinis enter the next generation, it is certain that Zia's "On the Hill" will remain a centerpiece for their family and a tradition enjoyed by the families of St. Louis for years to come.

# LINGUINE CARBONARA

### INGREDIENTS

*8 oz. linguine noodles cooked al dente*

*8 oz. cooked bacon, crumbled*

*¼ cup sliced fresh mushrooms*

*4 tbsp. butter*

*1 tsp. minced fresh garlic*

*1/8 tsp. cracked red pepper flakes*

*1/8 tsp. fresh ground black pepper*

*1 medium egg*

*8 oz. heavy whipping cream*

*Freshly grated Parmesan cheese*

Cook bacon in large skillet until crisp. Drain and crumble to equal 1 cup. Melt butter in large skillet. Add garlic, red pepper flakes, black pepper, bacon, and mushrooms. Saute over medium heat approximately 2-3 minutes. Add cream and bring to a full boil. Add linguine noodles and return to a full boil for approximately 2 minutes. Remove from heat. Add 1 egg and stir quickly to prevent from scrambling. Place in hot pasta bowls and top with freshly grated Parmesan cheese.

SERVES 2

*Zia (Aunt) Lena*

*Zia (Aunt) Anne*

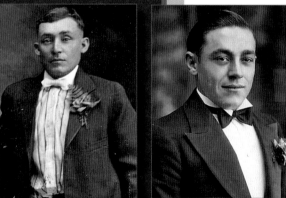

*Dennis and Angelo's grandfather, Angelo Chiodini.*

*Dennis and Angelo's father, Louis Chiodini.*

# PASTA TUTTOMARE

### INGREDIENTS

*8 oz. linguine*

*¼ cup (1/2 stick) butter*

*1 tsp. minced fresh garlic*

*1/8 tsp. red pepper flakes*

*1/8 tsp. freshly ground black pepper*

*Pinch of salt or to taste*

*2 oz. shrimp*

*2 oz. clams*

*4 oz. crabmeat (may substitute surimi sea legs)*

*¼ cup sliced mushrooms*

*8 oz. heavy whipping cream*

*Freshly grated Parmesan cheese and lemon wedge*

Cook linguine until al dente. Drain.

In a large skillet, melt butter. Cook garlic, red and black pepper, salt, shrimp, clams, crabmeat and mushrooms over medium-high heat, stirring occasionally, 2 to 3 minutes until seafood is fully cooked. Add cream. Bring to full boil. Add linguine. When mixture returns to full boil, cook about 2 minutes. Remove from heat and allow to rest.

Place pasta in warm pasta bowl. Top with Parmesan cheese and lemon wedge.

SERVES 1-2

*Angelo with his wife, Gerry, at their wedding in 1968.*

*Cory with Uncle Paul Chiodini.*

*Dennis' children: back row, Cory, Michelle, and Jason. Front row, Nick and "Rocky."*

*Robyn and Dennis Chiodini's wedding in June of 1971.*

200

# THE
# Perfect Italian Dinner *for Fall and Winter*

## BY DOMINIC GALATI

### APPETIZER OF SHRIMP

Begin meal with Prosecco or a dry, white wine with hors' d' oeuvres before bringing out appetizer. A simple dish to make, shrimp is a popular seafood which most people enjoy. Other seafoods can be used instead of shrimp.

### SPINACH SOUP WITH CHICKEN

The meal begins with a warm and comforting soup. It is broth-based, so it is light to the palate, yet the flavor is full and rich.

### FETTUCINE WITH SUN-DRIED TOMATOES, BASIL, AND PROSCIUTTO

It's important for a meal like this not to have any repetition in textures when serving all subsequent courses. A delicious tomato-based sauce gives a fresh, Mediterranean taste to the fettucine. At this point in time, add to the table a quality Italian, red wine.

### LEMON ICE WITH CAMPARI LIQUEUR

This course is the *Intermezzo* (Interlude). It refreshes and cleanses the palate. The Campari gives the ice a bitter, artichoke flavor.

### BROILED OR GRILLED FILET WITH WILD MUSHROOM SAUCE

As the main course, the beef tenderloin is an easy dish to produce and is a dependable choice. Combine with fresh, grilled vegetables (such as zucchini, tomato, asparagus, yellow squash) of your choice.

### INSALATA MISTA CON FORMAGGI

A traditional practice in Italy and Europe is to have cheese at this point. Plate the cheese with apples and toast as well as lettuce and nuts covered with a lemon-olive oil dressing.

### CRÈME BRULÉ

The Crème Brulé is an excellent and refreshing, but not overly sweet, ending to the meal. Easy to prepare, it can be made the day before serving and refrigerated. A dessert wine, such as Vino Santo, would be appropriate at this time.

202

# ANTIPASTO DI GAMBERO
# APPETIZER OF SHRIMP

### INGREDIENTS

*18 shrimp de-veined and peeled*

*1 cup mayonnaise*

*Juice of one lemon*

*¼ cup olive oil*

*2 tsp. brandy*

*2 tbsp. ketchup*

*1 bunch of leaf lettuce shredded*

*Salt and pepper to taste*

Boil shrimp for 8 minutes, and set aside. Put mayonnaise in a bowl. Add brandy, lemon, olive oil, ketchup, salt, and pepper to taste and stir well. Distribute a layer of shredded lettuce on plates. Mix sauce and shrimp together and place on top of lettuce. Refrigerate before serving

SERVES 4-6

---

# BRODO DI POLLO CON SPINACI
# CHICKEN SOUP WITH SPINACH

### INGREDIENTS

*3 tbsp. olive oil*

*¼ cup chopped onion*

*1 small carrot, chopped fine*

*2 breast of boneless, skinless chicken, diced*

*1 clove of fresh garlic, chopped*

*6 cups chicken bouillon*

*2 cups beef bouillon*

*Small handful fresh spinach, chopped*

*2 tbsp. minced parsley*

*1 tbsp. butter*

*Freshly ground black pepper to taste*

*Salt to taste*

*½ cup Romano cheese*

In a small pot, heat the oil and sauté carrot, onion, and garlic for five minutes. Add beef and chicken bouillon and let cook for five minutes. Bring to a boil and add chicken, spinach, and parsley. Cook for another five minutes until chicken is done. Add butter and season with salt and pepper and stir. Ladle soup into individual bowls, sprinkle with cheese and serve.

SERVES 6

# Fettucine con Pomodori Secchi
# Fettucine with Sun dried
# Tomatoes, Basil, and Prosciutto

### Ingredients

¼ cup olive oil

¼ cup onion, chopped fine

3 cloves of fresh garlic, chopped

¼ cup sun-dried tomatoes

3 oz. Prosciutto ham, cut into thin strips

2 large tomatoes peeled, seeded, and chopped

2 tbsp. butter

8 leaves of fresh basil, chopped

1 lb. fettucine

Salt and pepper to taste

½ cup grated Parmigiano cheese

Heat the oil in a sauce pan and sauté the onions and garlic until translucent. Add the sun-dried tomatoes, Prosciutto, and chopped tomatoes. Simmer for about six minutes. Reduce heat, and simmer for another 10 minutes. Add basil and butter and stir well.

Cook noodles in salted water for eight minutes or until al dente. Drain water, add noodles to the sauce, and mix together. Divide the pasta among the dishes, sprinkle with Parmigiano cheese and serve.

Serves 6

205

# Filetto con Salsa di Funghi
## Broiled or Grilled Filet with Wild Mushroom Sauce

### Ingredients

*2 lbs. beef tenderloin marinated overnight with olive oil,
   fresh garlic, pepper, and salt*

### Sauce

*6 tbsp. olive oil*

*2 large shallots, finely chopped*

*2 cloves of fresh garlic, chopped*

*1 small tomato peeled, seeded,
   and finely chopped*

*1 oz. pine nuts*

*1 cup wild mushrooms, chopped*

*1 oz. brandy*

*2 cups beef bouillon*

*½ cup heavy cream*

*2 tbsp. butter*

*2 tbsp. flour*

*1 pinch of fresh chopped parsley*

*Salt and pepper to taste*

Sauce: In a medium/large skillet, heat the oil and sauté shallots until translucent. Add garlic, tomato, pine nuts, and mushrooms and sauté for about five minutes. Add brandy, and let sauce simmer for about a minute until brandy evaporates. Add bouillon and cream. Roll the butter in the flour and add to sauce, (make sure you work the butter into the flour well). Turn down the heat and let sauce simmer until it thickens. Add parsley, salt, pepper, and set aside.

Broil or grill meat to the temperature desired. Slice meat in equal parts and set on plates. Before serving, spoon sauce on top of meat.

Serves 6

# Granite con Limone Campari
## Lemon Ice with Campari Liqueur

### Ingredients

*1 cup of sugar*

*3 cups of water*

*1 oz. Campari liqueur*

*¾ cup freshly squeezed lemon juice
   from 6 small lemons*

Make a syrup of the sugar, lemon, water, and Campari. Bring it to a boiling point, and cook just long enough to be sure sugar is completely dissolved. Allow to cool. Stir well, and pour into a shallow pan. Place in the freezer. After half an hour, remove from the freezer and scrape down the sides and bottom of the pan, breaking up the part that has solidified and blending it into that which is still liquid, until the granite comes to a fairly firm, flakey slush. Repeat this every 30 minutes until the consistency becomes solid.

Remove granite from the pan and serve.

Serves 4-6

## INSALATA MISTA CON FORMAGGI

INGREDIENTS

*¼ cup extra virgin olive oil*

*Juice of one lemon*

*6 small handfuls of mixed lettuce leaves*

*¼ cup walnuts*

*Salt and pepper*

*6 oz. Parmigiano Reggiano cheese, sliced*

*6 oz. imported Fontina cheese, sliced*

*12 thick slices of Italian bread, toasted on both sides*

*1 apple, cored and sliced*

In a small bowl, mix together the olive oil and lemon. In a bowl, place lettuce and walnuts. Add salt and pepper. Toss. Pour in lemon-oil dressing and toss gently. Arrange the salad on individual plates. Place the cheese, toast, apples on the side of the plate and serve.

SERVES 6

## CRÈME BRULÉ

INGREDIENTS

*2 cups whipping cream*

*4 tbsp. white sugar*

*4 egg yolks*

*1½ tbsp. vanilla extract*

*Brown sugar*

Preheat oven to 350 degrees. Scald whipping cream. Beat egg yolks with sugar and add vanilla to egg mixture. Slowly add scalded cream to egg mixture. Pour in ramekins and bake in a pan of hot water for 50 minutes. When done, sprinkle brown sugar on top. Run under the broiler for a few seconds until it looks burnt. Refrigerate and serve cold. Top with berries.

SERVES 6

# THE
# Perfect Italian Dinner *for Spring and Summer*

## BY CHARLIE GITTO, JR.

### PROSCIUTTO WITH MELON

The slight saltiness of the prosciutto paired with the cool and sweet melon makes a perfect summer starter. The dish is light enough not to fill you up and flavorful enough to whet your appetite for the rest of the meal.

### SICILIAN STUFFED ARTICHOKE

This classic Sicilian dish is one of my favorites. The flavors of the combination of the artichoke with garlic and olive oil are simple, yet pleasing.

### GRILLED SUMMER VEGETABLES

This fresh and light summer side is flavorful, thanks to the grilling preparation that brings out the natural sugars. This is a terrific way to make simple ingredients taste extraordinary.

### TOMATO EGGPLANT FRESH BUFFALO MOZZA-RELLA STACK

One of the greatest gifts of summer is a garden fresh tomato. We plant a restaurant garden every spring and anxiously wait for our plants to mature. This recipe is the perfect use for tomatoes, eggplant, and basil fresh from the garden.

### VEAL MILANESE

This classic is a very simple preparation, yet offers a rewarding texture and bright flavors of olive oil, parsley, and lemon.

### ZABAGLIONE WITH SUMMER BERRIES

This dessert is light and delicious! Zabaglione with a flavor of Marsala wine enhances the luscious, seasonal berries.

209

# GRILLED SUMMER VEGETABLES

INGREDIENTS

*2 yellow squash, sliced lengthwise, ¼-inch thick*

*2 zucchinis sliced lengthwise, ¼-inch thick*

*2 red bell peppers, stemmed, seeded, and sliced*
    *lengthwise into quarters*

*Extra virgin olive oil*

*Sea salt*

*Fresh ground black pepper*

Put all vegetables on a tray and drizzle with olive oil. Salt and pepper to taste. Grill vegetables until tender and slightly brown. Place on serving platter and drizzle with olive oil, salt, and pepper.

SERVES 6

# SICILIAN STUFFED ARTICHOKE

INGREDIENTS

*2 large artichokes*

*8 quarts water*

*2 tbsp. fresh lemon juice*

*¼ cup melted butter*

*1 clove minced garlic*

*¼ cup chopped fresh parsley*

*½ cup seasoned breadcrumbs*

*¼ cup grated Romano cheese*

Boil 8 quarts water with lemon juice. Blanche artichokes until tender. Remove choke and pointy ends of leaves. Melt butter, add garlic and cook slightly. Remove from heat. Set aside.

Stir the remaining ingredients and mix well. Fill each leaf of artichoke with breadcrumb mixture starting at the bottom. When ready to serve, wrap artichoke in plastic wrap and microwave on high for four minutes. Place on service piece and pour the garlic butter mixture over the top.

SERVES 6

# PROSCIUTTO WITH MELON

INGREDIENTS

*Crenshaw melon*

*½ lb. thinly sliced Prosciutto*

*Fresh mint sprigs*

*Lemon halves or wedges*

Cut ends off and peel melon. Scoop out seeds. Cut melon in half lengthwise. Slice into ¼-inch thick slices and place on a serving platter. Drape with thinly sliced Prosciutto and garnish with fresh mint and lemon.

SERVES 6

# Tomato Eggplant Fresh Buffalo Mozzarella Stack

### Ingredients

½ grilled eggplant sliced ¼-inch thick

9 tbsp. extra virgin olive oil

3 large homegrown tomatoes, sliced ¼-inch thick

¾ lb. fresh Mozzarella cheese, sliced ¼-inch thick

1 cup fresh basil leaves chiffonade
    (finely julienned)

Coarse sea salt

Freshly ground black pepper

3 tbsp. red wine vinegar

Pre heat outdoor grill. Place eggplant slices in a bowl and season with salt, pepper, and extra virgin olive oil. Place eggplant on grill and cook until tender, turning on both sides. Stack the salad in the following order – eggplant, tomato, and Mozzarella. Then repeat once. Season with sea salt and freshly ground pepper, and sprinkle with fresh basil. Drizzle the salad with red wine vinegar and add extra virgin olive oil. Add a side of buttered toast, garnished with parsley and serve.

Serves 6

# VEAL MILANESE

INGREDIENTS

*6 veal top round cutlets, cut 5 ounces each*

*2 cups Italian breadcrumbs*

*2 tbsp. chopped parsley*

*6 eggs beaten*

*½ cup olive oil*

*Salt*

*Freshly ground pepper*

Pound veal cutlets to ¼-inch thick. Season the veal cutlets with salt and pepper to taste. Dip the cutlets in egg, then into breadcrumb mixture. In a large skillet over medium heat, heat the oil. Cook the veal 1½ to 2 minutes per side. Serve on a platter garnished with lemon halves and parsley.

SERVES 6

# ZABAGLIONE WITH SUMMER BERRIES

INGREDIENTS

*1 pint fresh ripe blackberries*

*1 pint fresh raspberries*

*1 tbsp. sugar*

*2 tsp. lemon juice*

FOR THE ZABAGLIONE

*5 egg yolks*

*¾ cup sweet Marsala wine*

*½ cup sugar plus more to taste*

## THE BERRIES

Clean the berries and sprinkle with sugar and the lemon juice. Gently fold together to blend well. Set the berries aside to macerate.

## THE ZABAGLIONE

Begin by whisking to blend the yolks, Marsala wine, and sugar in a stainless steel bowl. Rest the bowl in a sauce pan over hot water. Whisk constantly for 4 to 5 minutes or more to cook the sauce, until it has the consistency of lightly whipped cream. When the mixture is thick, foamy, and triple in volume, remove from heat. Spoon berries into a glass and top with zabaglione. If desired, add more berries and more zabaglione to make three layers for each glass. Serve zabaglione tepid or cool.

SERVES 6

# ACKNOWLEDGEMENTS

First and foremost, I would like to thank the St. Louis Italian community who, as always, have embraced every new undertaking with enthusiasm. Their support and encouragement were key factors.

In particular, I would like to express appreciation to Monsignor Sal Polizzi, who wrote the book's Foreword and provided valuable information and photographs on Little Italy and the Hill. He served both parishes with devotion for many years. Also, thank you to Peter Rosciglione for encouraging us to bring to life the once-vibrant Little Italy community and his contribution to that section of the book.

I am deeply indebted to the numerous restaurants included for opening up their kitchens to our publication staff, sharing special family recipes, and allowing us to include their personal memoirs of family and times past. To those who spent long hours reminiscing with me, I am grateful; in particular, I thank Mickey Garagiola, Charlie Gitto, Sr., Dennis Chiodini, Rich LoRusso, Marty Ronzio, and the Meglio, Boccardi, and Imo families.

A big thanks to my niece, Faye Venegoni, for her support and editing skills. On the production end, thanks to Brad Baraks and his staff at G. Bradley Publishing for their expertise in creating this handsome publication; and to Jim Kersting, of Voyles Studio, for his exceptional color photography–the second time around! Last, but certainly not least, I'd like to give my heartfelt appreciation to my husband, Dominic, for his unending patience, encouragement, and his wonderful memory of people, places, and things past. If I've forgotten anyone who also shared their time and energy, please forgive me.

— Eleanore Berra Marfisi

*Foundry Field near Kingshighway witnesses the beginning of a St. Ambrose processional, led by Father Giovanni, through the Hill streets in the late 1920s.*

# CONTRIBUTORS

Mike Antinora
Patricia Ashman
Nicholas Belfiglio
Lance Berra
John and Rosemarie Bianchi
Scott Biondo
Joe Boccardi
Frank and Rosemarie Borghi
Harold Brazzle
Beverly Buck Brennan
Alyce Buck
Christine Buck
Agnes Carnaghi
Agnes Ceriotti
Dennis Chiodini
Ellen Cusumano

Jack Cusumano
Donna and Stephen
 Cusumano, O.D.
Aldo and Assunta
 Della Croce
Vincent DiRaimondo
John Favazza
Tony Favazza
Adrianna Fazio
Charles Gallagher, Sr.
Nina Ganci
Mickey Garagiola
Charlie Gitto, Sr.
Francesca Gitto
Stephen Gitto
Leo and Susan Grillo

Anna Jo Hof
Clarence Hughes
Joe Italian
Rosalie LaGates
Salvatore, Barbara,
 and Maria Licata
Anthony Lombardo
Rich LoRusso
Eugene Mariani
Tony and Jane Meglio
John Meglio
Patricia Merlo
John Mineo
Jean Moore
Patricia Nappier
Audrey Newcomer

Melodie Nicastro
Julia Pastore
Msgr. Salvatore Polizzi
Peter A. Puleo
Ambrose Ranzini
Peter, Pam, and
 Gina Rosciglione
Robert Ruggeri
Lucca Ruigi
Maria Sanfilippo
Tom Savio
Atty. Joseph Serra
Donald Shaw
Angelo Sita
Carol Stelzer
Kim Tucci

Faye Venegoni
Mario and Mary Ventucci
Peter and Grace Vitale
Scott K. Williams
Patrick Woodling


**Photo Contributors**
Collection of Mark I. Eisen-
 berg, St. Louis, Missouri
Archdiocese of St. Louis
 Archives
Missouri History Museum/
 Library and Research
 Center

# BIBLIOGRAPHY

Berra, Yogi. *I Really Didn't Say Everything I Said*. Workman Publishing Company. New York © 1998.

Berra, Yogi. *Ten Rings: My Championship Season*. Harper Collins. New York. © 2005.

Berra, Yogi. *When You Come to a Fork in the Road, Take It: Inspiration and Wisdom from One of Baseball's Greatest Heroes*. Hyperion. New York. © 2002.

Berra, Yogi. *Yogi…It Ain't Over*. HarperTorch. New York. © 1990.

Berra Marfisi, Eleanore. *The Hill: Its History, Its Recipes*. G. Bradley Publishing. St. Louis, Missouri. © 2003.

Berra Marfisi, Eleanore. *I Remember Nonna*. G. Bradley Publishing. St. Louis, Missouri. © 2004.

Buck, Jack. *Jack Buck: Forever a Winner*. Sports Publishing LLC. Champaign, IL. © 2003.

Buck, Jack. *That's a Winner*. Sagamore Publishing. Champaign, IL. © 1999.

Garagiola, Joe. *Baseball is a Funny Game*. J. B. Lippincott Company. Philadelphia/New York. © 1960.

Garagiola, Joe. *It's Anybody's Ballgame*. Bookthrift Co. © 1989.

Krantz, Les. *Reel Baseball: Baseball's Golden Era, the Way America Witnessed It – in the Movie Newsreels*. Doubleday. New York. © 2006.

Mormino, Gary Ross. *Immigrants on the Hill, Italian-Americans in St. Louis, 1882-1982*. University of Illinois Press. Urbana and Chicago. © 1986.

Schiavo, Giovanni [Ermenegildo]. *The Italians in Missouri*. Arno Press. New York. © 1975.

Wolfe, Rich. *Remembering Jack Buck: Wonderful Stories Celebrating the Life of a Broadcasting Legend*. American Institute of Excellence. © 2002.

*Historical Review, St. Ambrose Church–Fortieth Anniversary*. Boggiano Bros. © 1943.

http://www.thehillstl.com. Excerpts from the writings of Louis H. Schmidt.

# EPILOGUE

Our Italian ancestors were truly heroes. Part of the magic of their heroism was always their ability to embody a vision and to dare to make it happen. They are not just reflections of what has already been, rather they are harbingers of what WE may become.

It is imperative that we recognize the heroes of our heritage and to never allow their works and talents to be totally dissolved into the melting pot. They have bequeathed major contributions to the world in many fields. Among which are discoveries, explorations, art, entertainment, music, medicine, politics, science, sports, and of course, food.

Our own immigrant parents and grandparents were no less heroic than the dynamic men and women who have gone before them. Notwithstanding the difficulties our parents faced, which included lack of education, meager funds, language barriers, large families, they too, contributed to their new country. They and their sons have defended America in times of war; they have built homes in their neighborhoods giving added stability to their community. They have held positions in elected government offices, staffed hospitals, became educators, and instilled their children with a desire to learn, to work, and to share with the less fortunate.

So, today, we the sons and daughters of these brave immigrants must emulate their pride and passion. We must convey to the world that we who follow in the footsteps of our heroic Italian ancestors will promote the best and most notable of our heritage in this their new land, our native country–America.

> *"I've always believed that there was some plan that put this continent here to be found by people from every corner of the world who had the courage and the love of freedom enough to uproot themselves; leave family and friends and homeland, and come here to develop a whole new breed of people called Americans.*
>
> — Ronald Reagan